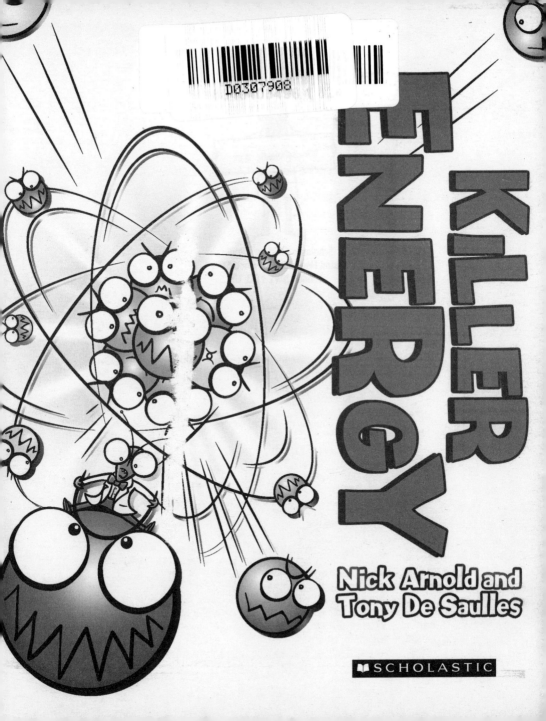

KILLER ENERGY

Nick Arnold and
Tony De Saulles

■SCHOLASTIC

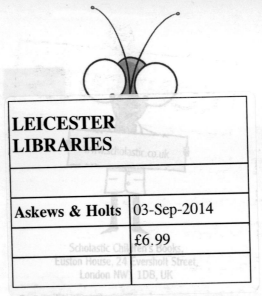

A division of Scholastic Ltd
London ~ New York ~ Toronto ~ Sydney ~ Auckland
Mexico City ~ New Delhi ~ Hong Kong

First published in the UK by Scholastic Ltd, 2001
This revised and updated edition published by Scholastic Ltd, 2014

Text copyright © Nick Arnold, 2001, 2014
Illustrations copyright © Tony De Saulles, 2001, 2014
Index by Caroline Hamilton

ISBN 978 1407 14449 8

Printed and bound by CPI Group (UK) Ltd, Croydon, CR0 4YY

2 4 6 8 10 9 7 5 3 1

CONTENTS

INTRODUCTION 5

THE ULTIMATE POWER 9

LAYING DOWN THE LAWS 17

HORRIBLE HEAT 35

THE DEAD FREEZING CHAPTER 52

KILLER COLD 63

HORRIBLY POWERFUL FUEL 81

THE POWER TO MOVE YOU 107

HOT, SWEATY BODY BITS 133

KILLER HEAT 155

FEARSOME FIERY FURNACES 174

A POWER FOR GOOD? 194

HORRIBLE INDEX 203

Nick Arnold has been writing stories and books since he was a youngster, but never dreamt he'd find fame writing about killer energy. His research involved building his own steam engine and entering an Iron Man Competition and he enjoyed every minute of it.

When he's not delving into Horrible Science, he spends his spare time eating pizza, riding his bike and thinking up corny jokes (though not all at the same time).

www.nickarnold-website.com

Tony De Saulles picked up his crayons when he was still in nappies and has been doodling ever since. He takes Horrible Science very seriously and even agreed to sketch radioactive atoms. Fortunately, he's made a full recovery. When he's not out with his sketchpad, Tony likes to write poetry and play squash, though he hasn't written any poetry about squash yet.

www.tonydesaulles.co.uk

INTRODUCTION

I hope you're not easily scared, because ... you're about to meet a huge, horribly powerful MONSTER!

PHROOM!

It's a very, very old monster (yes, it's even older than your science teacher). In fact, it's so incredibly ancient that it's as old as time itself. And the amazing thing about this monster is that it's always around but no one has ever seen it – *well not until now that is!*

The monster's name is ENERGY...

The Energy Monster gets everywhere. It makes stars shine and bonfires burn, and it moves everything from the slowest slug to the speediest spacecraft. But don't go thinking that the Energy Monster is a helpful gentle giant. No way! Take a deep breath and read on ... if you dare!

Sometimes the Energy Monster is a cruel, crazed, KILLER that destroys humans in hundreds of horrible ways. Of course, ordinary science books don't dwell on these disgusting details but this is a *Horrible Science* book – and that means you can read the killer energy info you *really* want to know, such as...

• Why this unlucky man is bursting into flames because of a fart...

• Why this man is gobbling foul fat in the snow...

• And why this scientist is getting rats drunk...

• Plus, the ULTIMATE FATE OF THE UNIVERSE (and whether it'll spoil your holiday this year).

HORRIBLE HEALTH WARNING!

This book contains foul facts, rude words and blood-thirsty cartoons. This material may shock teachers and other sensitive persons.

Hopefully, though, you're made of sterner stuff. Now, have you got enough energy to look over to the next page?

THE ULTIMATE POWER

Is your brain powered up? Well, this killer question will get it going so fast that steam could blast out of your ears. Ready? OK, here it is... *What do the following have in common?*

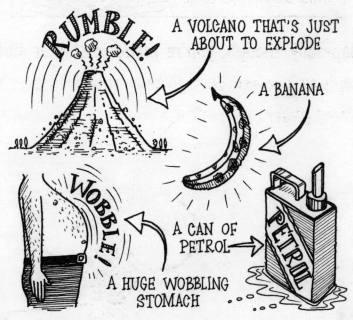

RUMBLE!

A VOLCANO THAT'S JUST ABOUT TO EXPLODE

A BANANA

WOBBLE!

A CAN OF PETROL →

PETROL

A HUGE WOBBLING STOMACH

Give up?

Well, they all store *energy*…

The volcano stores energy, which becomes movement energy when it erupts. And then you'll need lots of movement energy to run away. Bananas are great energy stores which is why some tennis players eat at least six every match. Petrol is a fuel so it's "fuel" of energy, and the bulging belly contains fat which is yet another food energy store…

Now at this point we were going to ask a teacher to tell us what energy is. But we couldn't find one who knew … see what I mean?

Honestly ... do I have to explain *everything* round here?

Killer energy fact file

Name: Energy

Basic facts: 1 Energy is the power that gets things moving. Since everything in the universe is moving, everything in the universe is powered by energy.

2 The word "energy" isn't too helpful – it just means "activity" in Greek.

IT'S ALL GREEK TO ME!

3 Energy takes many forms...

• Stored energy in fuel and food and other chemicals.

COAL

ENERGY STORED IN HERE

- Potential energy can be used in the future.

ROCK WILL HAVE ENERGY TO ROLL DOWN IN THE FUTURE.

- Movement energy

LET'S HOPE THE HUMAN HAS LOTS OF MOVEMENT ENERGY.

- Heat energy

HEAT IS A COMMON TYPE OF ENERGY.

And sound, light, electricity and magnetism are all types of energy too. Told you the Energy Monster gets everywhere!

Killer details:

Every execution method uses energy in one form or another. As you can see...

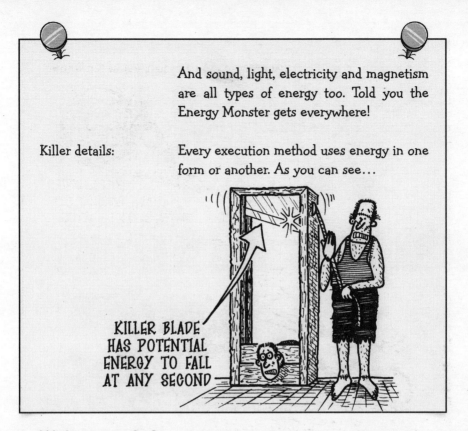

KILLER BLADE
HAS POTENTIAL
ENERGY TO FALL
AT ANY SECOND

With me so far?

So energy gets things moving and takes different forms. But someone had to figure this out. As you can imagine, scientists in the past had some really wrong ideas about energy. Here are four scientists to argue their points of view...

THE GREAT ENERGY DEBATE

Famous Greek philosopher, **Aristotle** (384–322 BC)

Not-so-famous Greek philosopher, **Anaxagoras** (500–428 BC)

German scientist, philosopher, mathematician, historian and all-round know-all, **Gottfried Leibniz** (1646–1716)

German scientist, **Georg Ernst Stahl** (1660–1734)

Things have the energy to move because they are guided by a great unseen mind called the nous.

That's rubbish — an invisible substance called pneuma makes things move.

These ideas were as sensible as attacking a lion's mane with a razor, running five miles to escape, and then shouting: "HOW'S THAT FOR A CLOSE SHAVE!"

It took scientists until the 1850s for a number of them (working separately) to begin to make scientific sense of energy. And then they came up with the Laws of Thermodynamics (that's ther-mo-dy-nam-ics). And if you thought I said "thermal underwear" you really need to read the next chapter to find out what the heck I'm going on about…

LAYING DOWN THE LAWS

In this chapter you'll find out about the Laws of Thermodynamics. They sound dead posh and impressive but actually they're horribly easy to understand. (Don't tell anyone how easy, and with luck your friends will think you are a scientific genius!)

Killer energy fact file

Name: The Laws of Thermodynamics

Basic facts: 1 "Thermodynamics" means "moving heat". The laws tell you what heat energy does and how it links up with other forms of energy.

2 By the way, when a scientist talks about "laws" they don't mean rules like "PLEASE DON'T CHEW YOUR TEACHER'S LEG IN SCIENCE LESSONS". They mean scientific explanations proven by lots of experiments.

3 Try to break the Laws of Thermodynamics and you'll find...

a) It's impossible...

b) You'll be laughed at by a heartless gang of scientists who knew it was impossible but didn't warn you because they wanted to watch you make a fool of yourself.

Killer details: The search for these laws drove one scientist into madness. Let's hope you're more fortunate...

THERMO DIE MANIC! DON'T PANIC! RAVE! JIBBER!

SO, WHAT DO THE LAWS SAY?

Meet Harvey Tucker, the biggest journalist in Australia – well, he's certainly the largest (and the laziest).

G'DAY SPORTS!

Later on he'll be investigating energy (that's if he can be bothered). But for now, we've managed to persuade Harvey to report on how the Laws work…

THE LAWS OF THERMODYNAMICS

Well, I wasn't too hot on thermo … heat energy, but no worries – I surfed stacks of info from the Internet.

19

Phew – it's hard yakka! Anyway, here's the low-down...

LAW ONE
Energy can't be made or destroyed. But heat energy can be used to power movement energy and movement energy can turn into heat energy. Streuth! That's fair dinkums. If I did some work I'd have more movement energy and this would make me feel more heat energy. So I'd best sit here with my lager and save my energy – BURP!

HEAT ENERGY → POWERS → MOVEMENT ENERGY

CAN TURN INTO

LAW TWO
Heat energy always moves from hot things to cold things. So heat from the sun is warming up my cold lager. Well, talk about stating the blithering obvious! If heat went from cold places to hot places my lager would cool down in the sun – well, that would be the day! I'm fair cooked already!

HOT SUN

HEAT ALWAYS MOVES IN THIS DIRECTION

COLD BEER

LAW THREE

You can't get colder than -273.16°C (-459.67°F) - otherwise known as **ABSOLUTE ZERO**. The scientists say when something's this cold it ain't got no heat energy! Lucky it doesn't get that cold in Oz - I do feel the cold, see?

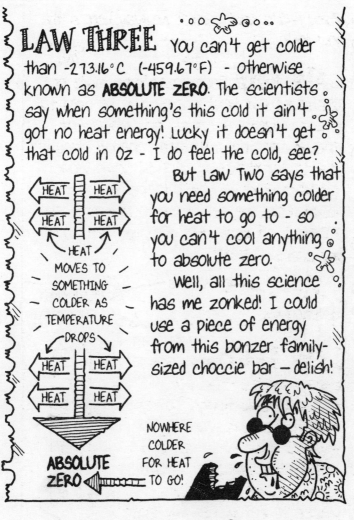

HEAT HEAT
HEAT HEAT

HEAT MOVES TO SOMETHING COLDER AS TEMPERATURE DROPS

HEAT HEAT
HEAT HEAT

ABSOLUTE ZERO

NOWHERE COLDER FOR HEAT TO GO!

But Law Two says that you need something colder for heat to go to - so you can't cool anything to absolute zero.

Well, all this science has me zonked! I could use a piece of energy from this bonzer family-sized choccie bar – delish!

We'll be taking a look at Laws Two and Three in the next two chapters, but for now we'll stick to Law One. Did you know that a scientist who worked on the first law got his ideas from *blood*? Yes, it's true!

Read on for the bloodthirsty details…

Hall of Fame: Julius Robert von Mayer (1814–1878)
Nationality: German

"Ach mein Gott – I hev cut an artery! Hold still or you vill bleed to death!"

As he spoke, the young doctor turned white and his hands began to shake as he held the bowl to the sailor's brawny arm. The bowl was steadily filling with blood. Bright red, glistening blood, the kind that squirts from the heart through the high-pressure arteries.

But the sailor's face crinkled into a weak smile. It was a pained smile because the blood was still draining from his arm and he was exhausted from fever.

"Don't you fret, doc – our blood always comes out this red in these parts. I don't understand it, mind, but there it is."

With his mind racing, the doctor set down the bowl of blood. Then he bandaged the crewman's arm with a grubby strip of material to staunch the blood that was still trickling from his arm.

In 1840 doctors like Mayer believed the best way to treat disease was to drain blood from their patients' veins. But when Julius tried to do this in Java he found the blood was bright red, even in veins where it's usually dark red. Julius Mayer was about to make a great discovery.

It nearly destroyed him.

Julius was not a lucky person. He didn't do well at school and he was expelled from university for joining a secret club that was frowned on by his teachers. (Today's teachers are a bit more understanding, so you may escape being expelled for joining the Horrible Club.)

Mayer was allowed back into university the following year. He studied medicine and became a ship's doctor – and that's how he came to be in

Java in 1840. Seeing the red blood got him thinking. Here's how Mayer might have made sense of the puzzle in letters to his best friend – his brother…

Jakarta, Java 1841

Dear Fritz,

Remember the red blood I mentioned in my last letter? I do, I can't stop thinking about it, and now I've got an idea!

1. Bright red blood contains oxygen. The body needs oxygen in order to live – that's why we breathe!

2. The blood in the sailor's veins was bright red with oxygen. Since veins carry blood back from the body this means the sailor's body is using less oxygen than usual.

OXYGEN

3. I think the body uses oxygen to keep warm. But when it's hot (like here — sorry about the sweat stains!) the body needs less heat so it uses less oxygen. Yes, I think I've cracked it! What do you think?
Your bruv,
   Jools

MORE OXYGEN

LESS OXYGEN

Jakarta, Java 1841
Hi Fritz,
It's me again...
Don't know what's got into me — but I've suddenly had loads of WONDERFUL NEW IDEAS!

1. I think the body needs food as well as oxygen to make heat. It's a bit like a fire that needs fuel and oxygen to burn properly.

FOOD + OXYGEN

2. This means energy must switch from one form to another. Yes, I reckon energy must be stored in food and turn into heat and movement energy inside the body.

Am I hot on the trail — or is my brain over-heating? I can't wait to get home and tell everyone!
Your very excited bruv,
Jools

ENERGY

ENERGY

YIPPEEE

Mayer was right not once but TWICE!! He'd made not one but TWO brilliant breakthroughs! He'd figured how the body uses energy *and* he'd got the idea for the First Law of Thermodynamics. (Remember, it showed the link between heat and movement energy.) Of course, all the other scientists were thrilled and Jools became famous and lived happily ever after ... didn't he?

Excuse me – this is Horrible Science not some sloppy-soppy little fairy tale! Mayer wrote an article and sent it to a science magazine but they didn't reply. No one believed him because he hadn't done any experiments to prove his ideas. So Mayer studied science for months and months until he knew enough to re-write the article in more scientific language. But by the time the article was published, other scientists had put forward the same idea. There were heated rows over who'd thought of the First Law first...

BET YOU NEVER KNEW!

1 One of the rival scientists was a Briton, James Joule (1818–1889). James's family was so rich he never had to go to school. He even had a top scientist, John Dalton (1766–1844), as his very own personal teacher.

AND I'D LIKE THE NEXT THREE WEEKS OFF, DALTON!

YES, CERTAINLY MASTER JAMES

(You could ask your parents to let you off school and pay for your own teacher, and if you happen to be dreaming they might even say "YES!")

2 James had a private lab for energy experiments. In 1843 he found out, by measuring the temperature of water turned by a paddle, that movement energy can be turned into heat energy.

3 Today, scientists measure energy in joules. One joule gives you enough energy to lift an apple one metre – can you do this?

Now back to miserable Mayer…

Julius Mayer's luck hadn't turned. He fell in love and got married but five of his seven children died of disease. Revolution broke out in Germany, and Fritz supported the revolution, but Julius was arrested for opposing it. He was soon released but fell out with his brother. Julius grew increasingly miserable about his lack of scientific success. One unhappy day, he decided to take his own life. He failed but his family thought he was mad and he spent ten years locked in mental hospitals.

I'VE JUST DISCOVERED THE FOURTH LAW OF THERMODYNAMICS — **DON'T TELL ANYBODY ABOUT THE FIRST THREE!**

It was only years later that scientists came to realize that the First Law of Thermodynamics was correct. At last, when Mayer was a broken old man, Britain's top scientists at the Royal Society awarded him a gold medal. But talking about the First Law – here's an experiment that shows it in action. Go on, give it a go – it's easy!

DARE YOU DISCOVER ... THE FIRST LAW OF THERMODYNAMICS?

You will need:

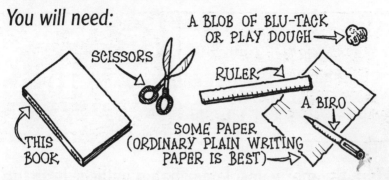

What you do:

1 Place the paper over this shape and trace round it. Draw in the fold line using the ruler.

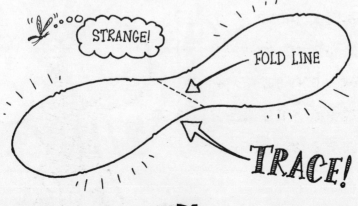

2 Cut out the shape you've drawn. DON'T cut out the shape from your Horrible Science book, *especially* if it comes from the library! Fold one side of the shape along the line. Unfold the shape.

3 Stick the Blu-Tack on a table and stick the pen in it, so it's standing on end. Make sure the pen is upright (use the ruler to check).

4 Turn the shape upside down and balance it on the point of the biro so that the sides point downwards at about 45° – carefully does it!

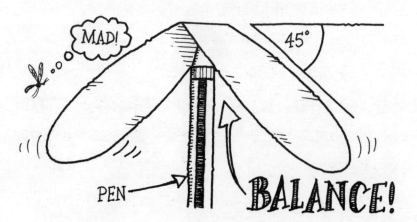

MAD!

45°

PEN

BALANCE!

5 Watch what happens to the shape for a minute or two. Then place your hands on their sides on the table to make a circle round the biro. (If your hands are cold you need to rub them until they're warm.)

HEAT! HEAT!

WACKO!

TOTALLY BONKERS!

What do you notice?

a) The shape rocks backwards and forwards.

b) The shape whizzes into the air.

c) The shape moves around and then stops. When I put my hands near it the shape moves round faster than before.

ANSWER

c) The shape is powered by heat energy! It might move at first because of draughts in the room or wobble as it balances on top of the pen. But it really gets going when the hot air rises off your hands. This proves the First Law is right when it says that heat energy can make things move.

But talking about heat – it just so happens that the next chapter is all about this cosy topic ... will you warm to it?

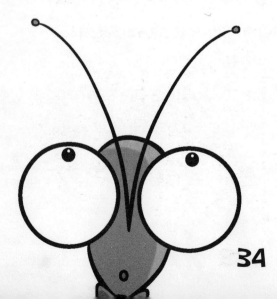

HORRIBLE HEAT

This chapter lets you into some sizzling heat secrets, including how the Second Law affects the entire universe and how an extremely important sausage changed the course of history...

What's that? You don't remember what the Second Law says? Well, it's the one that says heat energy goes from a hot object to a cooler area. And actually, come to think of it, the Second Law actually sneaked into that experiment in the last chapter.

IN THE EXPERIMENT HEAT ENERGY PASSED FROM A HOT AREA — YOUR HOT, STICKY HANDS — TO A COOLER AREA — THE AIR.

YIKES!

And as I said, the Second Law has a HUGE effect on the whole universe.

Take this nice hot cup of tea…

IS MY TEA READY YET?

The Second Law says all the time the cup of tea is losing heat energy. In other words, it's cooling down. If you blow on the tea, it will cool even faster.

Your breath blows away the air warmed by the hot tea and the heat energy flows more quickly into the cooler air.

BLOW!

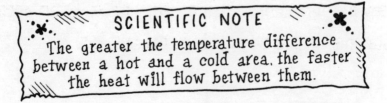

SCIENTIFIC NOTE

The greater the temperature difference between a hot and a cold area, the faster the heat will flow between them.

In half an hour the tea is disgustingly lukewarm.

In an hour, it's stone cold.

The only way to make the tea hot is to heat it up again – in other words to add more heat energy!

And what's true for the tea is also true for everything in the *entire universe*. Yes, the Second Law says that *everything*, from galaxies to gravy, from hippos to hotwater bottles, is forever cooling down. Your body is losing heat and so is an alien starship on the other side of the cosmos.

*WE'RE LOSING
HEAT, CAPTAIN!

*IT'S THAT BLASTED
2ND LAW, AGAIN!

And the only way to keep anything hot is to chuck in more heat energy. And that means you'd better eat your dad's revolting rice pudding and digest it and turn it into heat to replace the heat energy you lost today.

And that rotten old Second Law has some even worse news for you on page 196. But first it's time to find out a bit more about a real hot topic...

Killer energy fact file

Name:

Basic facts:

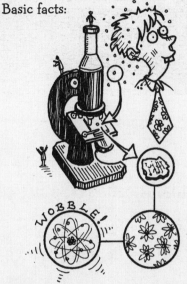

Killer details:

Heat energy

1 If you looked at a speck of dandruff through a super-powerful microscope (yes, more powerful than any microscope in the world) you'd see the tiny atoms that make it up.

2 The atoms are wobbling. This movement is what we call heat energy and the hotter the atoms are the faster they wobble. With me so far?

1 At absolute zero (-273°C) they can't move, not even an itsy-bitsy mini-wobble. The atoms have no heat energy at all.

2 Very low temperatures can preserve dead bodies forever – (page 59 will send a cold shiver down your spine).

NOT SO HOT THEORIES...

You can't expect scientists to grasp all this straight away and early ideas about heat were definitely on the tepid side. Here's Swiss scientist Pierre Prévost (1751–1839).

Of course this "caloric" was a load of hot air, but Prévost wasn't proved wrong until American scientist Benjamin Thompson, Count Rumford

(1753–1814), took on a boring job. He worked as Minister for War in Bavaria, Germany, and he was watching a cannon being bored by a drill. The cannon got very hot and, if you believed in caloric, you might think that the cannon would run out of the hot stuff after a while. But it didn't!

So Rumford realized that heat can't be a substance – it must be a form of energy that was picked up from the rubbing of the drill in the same way that rubbing your hands makes them feel warmer. In 1798 Rumford proudly announced his discovery at a meeting of the Royal Society and … no one took any notice.

I bet they were even more *bored* than the cannon…

TERRIBLY TACKY THERMOMETERS

The measurement of heat energy is called temperature (I hope you're suitably impressed by this fact). But early scientists had a problem measuring heat as no one had got around to inventing the thermometer. After combing dozens of scientific junk shops we've uncovered a selection of ancient thermometers...

Ye Olde Scientific Junk Shop

SALE TODAY

LET'S HOPE YOUR SCHOOL EQUIPMENT ISN'T THIS OLD — EVEN IF YOUR SCIENCE TEACHER MIGHT BE.

Air-filled thermoscope invented by Italian genius Galileo Galilei (1564-1642) - uses air and water to measure temperature.

Albert Einstein's eyeballs

Galileo's skull

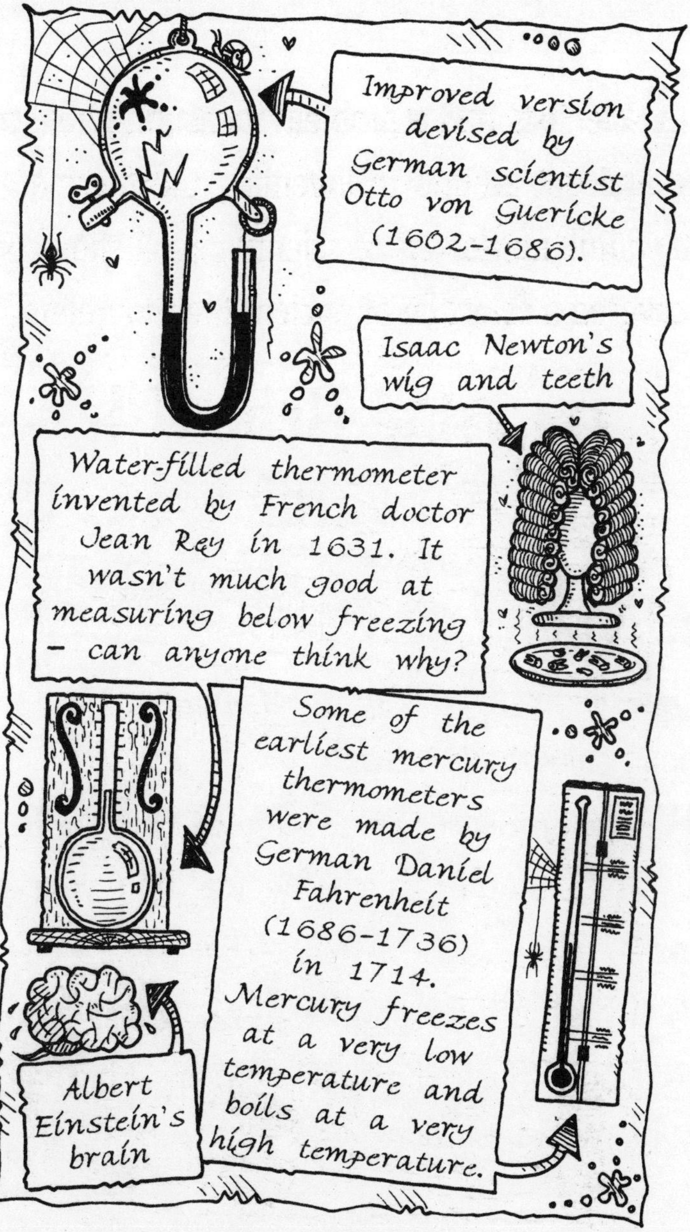

Improved version devised by German scientist Otto von Guericke (1602–1686).

Isaac Newton's wig and teeth

Water-filled thermometer invented by French doctor Jean Rey in 1631. It wasn't much good at measuring below freezing – can anyone think why?

Some of the earliest mercury thermometers were made by German Daniel Fahrenheit (1686–1736) in 1714. Mercury freezes at a very low temperature and boils at a very high temperature.

Albert Einstein's brain

DARE YOU DISCOVER ... HOW TO MAKE YOUR OWN THERMOSCOPE?

You will need:

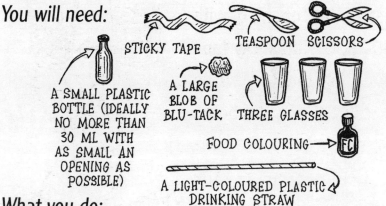

STICKY TAPE   TEASPOON   SCISSORS

A SMALL PLASTIC BOTTLE (IDEALLY NO MORE THAN 30 ML WITH AS SMALL AN OPENING AS POSSIBLE)

A LARGE BLOB OF BLU-TACK   THREE GLASSES

FOOD COLOURING → FC

A LIGHT-COLOURED PLASTIC DRINKING STRAW

What you do:

1 Half-fill one glass with water and add a few drops of food colouring. Stir well.

2 Half-fill the second glass with ice from the freezer (be careful not to touch the ice with your bare hands).

3 Half-fill the third glass with hot water from the tap. (Don't touch the water either – it could be scalding!)

4 Stick the straw in the bottle and block up the rest of the opening with Blu-Tack. Wrap sticky tape round the Blu-Tack so no air can get into the bottle except through the straw.

5 Gently squeeze the bottle and turn it upside down so the end of the straw is in the coloured water. Coloured water will flow up the straw. Now stop squeezing the bottle and put it the right way up. You should see a band of coloured water in the straw.

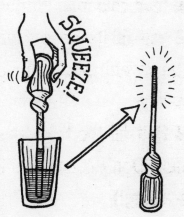

6 Place the bottle in the glass of ice and then in the hot water.

What do you notice?

a) The water in the straw goes up in the ice and down in the hot water.

b) The water in the straw goes up in the hot water and down in the ice.

c) The water in the straw becomes lighter in the ice and darker in the hot water.

ANSWER

b) Remember those wobbling atoms on page 39? When you heat up the air in the bottle, the atoms have energy and try to move off in all directions — think of a class of energetic kids running outside at break-time.

The warm air atoms push up the straw and they push the water up too. When the air is cold the atoms have less heat energy so they don't want to go anywhere – think of kids huddling together for warmth on a cold day.

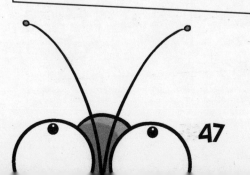

The pressure of the air pushing down on the straw from above pushes the water level down.

BET YOU NEVER KNEW!

The plans of Galileo's thermoscope were amongst his papers when the great man died. Galileo left his papers to scientist, Vincenzo Viviani (1622–1703). But when Viviani died, his family thought the papers were worthless rubbish, so they sold them to a local sausage maker to wrap his bangers. Then another scientist ate one of the sausages and read the writing on the wrapper. He bought the entire stock of wrappers including the designs for the thermoscope. And so it was that Galileo's great discoveries were saved – thanks to a sausage.

TRICKY TEMPERATURE FACTS

1 Scientists still had a problem. They had thermometers but they couldn't agree on a scale to measure temperature. Scientists made up their own measurements – and this no doubt led to heated arguments.

2 The first widely used measure of temperature was invented by our pal Daniel Fahrenheit – can you guess what it was called?

3 Fahrenheit decided that the coldest temperature he could make by mixing chemicals in his lab was 0°. This meant that water froze at 32° and the temperature of the human body was 96° (that's three times 32°). But Fahrenheit hadn't got it right – the body is around 98.6° so his carefully planned scale was wrong.

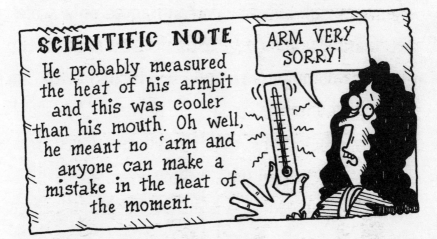

SCIENTIFIC NOTE
He probably measured the heat of his armpit and this was cooler than his mouth. Oh well, he meant no 'arm and anyone can make a mistake in the heat of the moment.

ARM VERY SORRY!

4 Fahrenheit's scale is now used in the USA but the rest of the world uses a measurement invented by a Swedish scientist named Anders Celsius (1701–1744). It's sometimes called centigrade but the official name is the Celsius scale after its inventor.

Anders was the son of a Professor of Astronomy and he grew up interested in maths and science. He loved exploring and went on two trips to the north of Finland. There he studied the Northern Lights and made observations that proved the Earth was slightly flattened at the North Pole.

5 Anders suggested a scale of 100° with water boiling at 0° and ice melting at 100°. Yes, you did read that right – Anders Celsius put his scale the wrong way round but another scientist reversed it after his death. Oh well, I guess they had a "measured" approach to science.

But talking about freezing, there's lots of freezing going on in the next chapter. In fact the next chapter's cold enough to freeze a cup of tea rock-hard *in one millisecond!*

Are you wrapped up *really* warm?

AND DON'T FORGET YOUR SCARF!

OH NO – MUM!

THE DEAD FREEZING CHAPTER

If science leaves you cold you might be gob-smacked to hear that science really can be cool – in fact *supercool!* Yes, this chapter and the next one are about losing heat energy and the science of low temperatures.

THE BIG FREEZE-UP

Remember the Third Law of Thermodynamics – the one that says that you can't get colder than absolute zero? (See page 19 if you don't.) Bet you never knew that one scientist who worked on this law went to university when he was just *ten years old*. He's been dead for ages but we've zapped him with energy for one last interview…

DEAD BRAINY: WILLIAM THOMSON, LORD KELVIN (1824-1907)

Welcome back to the land of the living, your lordship.

IT'S GOOD TO BE BACK!

So what's it like to be dead?

I'M BURIED IN LONDON IN WESTMINSTER ABBEY NEXT TO ISAAC NEWTON. I'M HAPPY TO BE SEEN DEAD WITH HIM...

You began your career by going to university at the age of ten.

WELL, I'M NOT ONE TO BOAST BUT SCHOOL SCIENCE WAS JUST TOO EASY FOR ONE OF MY GIANT INTELLECT.

Your first maths discovery was read to a science meeting by someone else — why didn't you read it yourself?

I WAS ONLY TEN AT THE TIME — IT MUST HAVE BEEN PAST MY BED-TIME.

You eventually became a Professor at Glasgow University...

me talking to a student

YES, I WAS GETTING ON A BIT BY THEN — I WAS ALL OF 22

And how long did you stick the job?

1842 1899

FIFTY-THREE YEARS — UNTIL I RAN OUT OF ENERGY

You studied electricity and heat and worked on the Second and Third Laws of Thermodynamics...

YES, THEY WERE BEING HOTLY DEBATED AT THE TIME.

Using maths you calculated that you couldn't cool anything below absolute zero.

0° KELVIN

YES, IT'S KNOWN AS 0° KELVIN — GOOD NAME, EH?

You advised on the laying of the first telegraph cable across the Atlantic Ocean and made a fortune.

YES, I WAS "CABLE" TO ANSWER EVERY QUESTION.

Of course, you made some mistakes in your scientific work...

EH?

You claimed that the sun's heat comes from burning coal.

I WONDER IF IT'S RUN OUT YET?

BET YOU NEVER KNEW!

1 A degree on the Kelvin scale is the same as a degree Celsius but unlike Celsius, the Kelvin scale starts at absolute zero. The scale is used for scientific measurements of the heat energy of atoms and it's named after the great man because he suggested it.

2 Thomson was made Lord Kelvin for his services to science. He took his title from a small river in Glasgow (I expect the locals call it "a wee burn"). So today scientists use the name of a wee burn in Scotland every time they measure temperature.

SPOT THE DIFFERENCES...

THE KELVIN — A WEE BURN

A HOT PLATE WITH A LOT OF KELVIN

LORD KELVIN WITH A WEE BURN

WELCOME TO THE CHILL-OUT ZONE

So would you like to experience absolute zero (almost)? Well, what you need is a holiday in space...

BET YOU NEVER KNEW!

Away from the sun's heat, space is only a degree or two above absolute zero. It's so cold that pee ejected from a space loo freezes instantly into a pretty stream of golden crystals. When asked what was the most beautiful sight he had seen, one returning astronaut replied:

THE URINE DUMP AT SUNSET

For some chilled-out scientists this sort of thing is brrrrrilliant. They cool atoms for super-cool experiments by trapping them with magnetic forces. Did you know that electricity runs through the chilled-out atoms with scarcely any friction? Well that's just the start of the weird stuff...

THE ICE IS NICE COMPANY

P R E S E N T S...

Fancy a cool thrill?

COOL!

Buy this super-cooled helium (it's the same gas they put in high-flying balloons) but it's cooled to −272.2° C (−485° F).

Amaze your friends and terrify the cat as it turns into a liquid and starts climbing the sides of the jar.

THE SMALL PRINT
Don't drop your cat in the helium or you might end up with a frozen pet!

Fancy an ice cream?

Can't wait hours for it to freeze? Try using this super-cold liquid nitrogen at −196° C (−393° F)! In 1997 a British scientist used this substance to make ice cream in ten seconds! Children who sampled the ice cream said it was "very nice" and a chef said:

IT'S NOT VERY RICH OR CREAMY, BUT IT DEFINITELY TASTES LIKE AN ICE CREAM.

THE SMALL PRINT
The nitrogen won't spoil the taste. When it meets air it turns into nitrogen gas and floats away – and that's fine, because air is mostly nitrogen gas.

57

By the way, if you're thinking of making the ice cream you should know that if you stick your finger in liquid nitrogen it'll freeze solid and break off. I guess that's what they call "a cold snap" – or do I mean ice-scream?

But talking about dipping bodies in liquid nitrogen, did you know that some people are planning to preserve their dead bodies in just this fashion?

Fearless reporter Harvey Tucker is just about to find out more…

HARVEY TUCKER'S BIG ADVENTURE

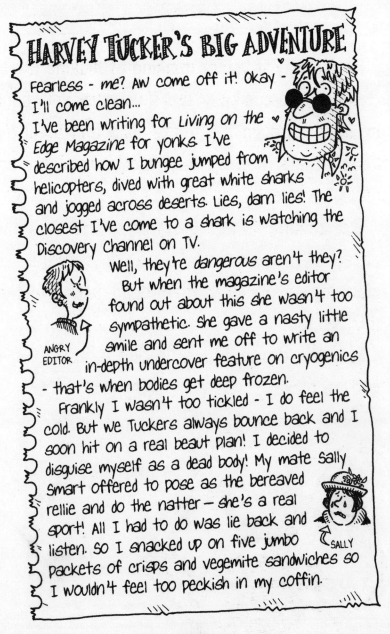

Fearless - me? Aw come off it! Okay - I'll come clean....

I've been writing for *Living on the Edge Magazine* for yonks. I've described how I bungee jumped from helicopters, dived with great white sharks and jogged across deserts. Lies, darn lies! The closest I've come to a shark is watching the Discovery Channel on TV.

Well, they're dangerous aren't they?

But when the magazine's editor found out about this she wasn't too sympathetic. She gave a nasty little smile and sent me off to write an in-depth undercover feature on cryogenics - that's when bodies get deep frozen.

ANGRY EDITOR

Frankly I wasn't too tickled - I do feel the cold. But we Tuckers always bounce back and I soon hit on a real beaut plan! I decided to disguise myself as a dead body! My mate Sally Smart offered to pose as the bereaved rellie and do the natter - she's a real sport! All I had to do was lie back and listen. So I snacked up on five jumbo packets of crisps and vegemite sandwiches so I wouldn't feel too peckish in my coffin.

SALLY

So there I was at the body store of the Frozen Funerals company concentrating on being dead.

"What we do," said the doc, "is drain the body of blood and fill it up with antifreeze and other chemicals..."

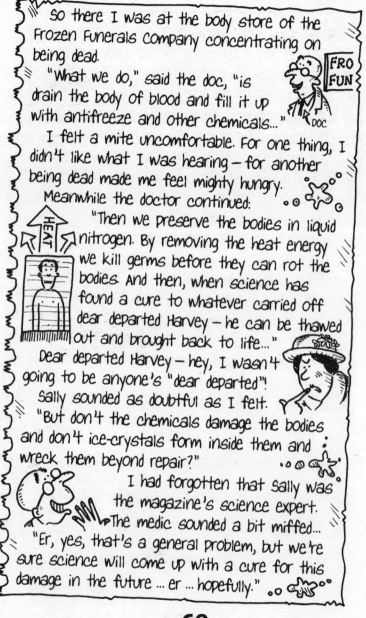

I felt a mite uncomfortable. For one thing, I didn't like what I was hearing — for another being dead made me feel mighty hungry.

Meanwhile the doctor continued:

"Then we preserve the bodies in liquid nitrogen. By removing the heat energy we kill germs before they can rot the bodies. And then, when science has found a cure to whatever carried off dear departed Harvey — he can be thawed out and brought back to life..."

Dear departed Harvey — hey, I wasn't going to be anyone's "dear departed"!

Sally sounded as doubtful as I felt.

"But don't the chemicals damage the bodies and don't ice-crystals form inside them and wreck them beyond repair?"

I had forgotten that Sally was the magazine's science expert. The medic sounded a bit miffed...

"Er, yes, that's a general problem, but we're sure science will come up with a cure for this damage in the future ... er ... hopefully."

Whilst they were yacking, I risked opening an eye and taking a butchers at the body store. I could see bodies in flasks – a chill ran through my veins.

I felt as cold as the bods.

"How much does it cost?" Sally was asking.

"That depends," replied the doc. "It's $100,000 for the full body but only $50,000 for the head – it's a cut-price offer."

Cut off – what?! Well, I freaked didn't I?

"Forget it, mate!" I yelled sitting up in my coffin.

ARGH!

The doctor screamed and ran off and Sally gave me a frosty look. She's been really cold to me ever since.

Cryogenics is popular in the USA and many bodies and heads have already been frozen. Some people have had their pet dogs preserved – I guess they're frozen Fidos. But some companies operating the service have gone bust and had their assets frozen (maybe it's the chilly economic climate) and the bodies thawed out with smelly results. I'm sure it's a thaw point all round.

Of course, you don't need to find a vat of liquid nitrogen to find a frozen body – there are plenty of well-preserved bodies in the polar regions at the ends of the Earth. Why not turn to the next ice-cool chapter and find out how they got there and what happens to the body when it gets low on vital heat energy. Yes, read on, you're about to make a chilling discovery…

KILLER COLD

This chapter is warmer than the last one, but it's still freezing cold. Later chapters will be hot enough to fry your fingertips but for now you're more likely to freeze them off! This chapter is full of cool killer facts about how lack of heat energy freezes water ... and people.

COULD YOU BE A SURGEON?

You're a surgeon. Your patient has a swelling blood vessel in his brain. Soon the blood vessel will burst and cause a killer build up of blood pressure. Your patient could die — what can you do? Better hurry up and decide...

a) Cut open the patient's skull and squirt the brain with liquid nitrogen to freeze  it up and stop the blood moving.

b) Cut open the skull and pack ice cubes around the brain to reduce the swelling.

c) Pack the patient's body with ice until their body temperature is low, remove half their blood and then operate on the brain.

c) Cooling the body slows it down so it needs less oxygen from the blood. (In fact, cooling can be used to treat severely injured people by giving their bodies a chance to heal naturally.) By draining the blood you reduce swelling and gain time to operate on the blood vessel. In the 1960s a Japanese brain surgeon chilled the brains of patients to 6°C (43°F), drained their blood and operated before warming the brains up with nice hot blood. I expect he needed a cool head.

BET YOU NEVER KNEW!

In 1983 a temperature of -89.2°C (-128.6°F) was recorded at the Russian Vostock Base, Antarctica. This was so cold that if you threw a mug of boiling tea in the air it would turn into a tea-flavoured ice lolly before it hit the ground!

Fancy going there for a holiday? Well, if so you'll enjoy chilling out in a hotel built out of solid ice! There really is such a place ... here's how they might advertise it.

So what's this got to do with energy?

Killer energy fact file

Basic facts:

Killer details:

1 As water cools it loses heat energy to the air.

2 At 0°C (32°F) the groups of atoms (molecules as scientist call them) that make up water lock together.

3 Ice still has heat energy and the frozen water molecules are still gently wobbling.

1 If you added up all the heat energy in an ice cube there'd be enough to produce a flame hotter than a burning match.

2 When you make a snowball you crush the ice-crystals together and this movement energy turns to heat energy that melts some of the ice. The squishy water makes the ball easy to mould. BEWARE – if the snowball hits your teacher he might go in for the kill!

HORRIBLE HEALTH WARNING!

And talking about danger – ice freezes from the edges of a pond but walking on ice is horribly risky! You could find yourself in a hole lot of DANGER!

ARGH!

HAVE AN ICE DIP!

TEACHER'S TEA-BREAK TEASER

It's break-time. With luck your teacher will just be getting some milk from the fridge to put in her tea when you knock on the staffroom door...

IF THE SECOND LAW OF THERMODYNAMICS SAYS HEAT ALWAYS GOES FROM A WARM PLACE TO A COLD PLACE, HOW IS IT POSSIBLE FOR FRIDGES TO MOVE HEAT OUT FROM THE COLD FRIDGE TO THE WARM ROOM?

WHAT?

ANSWER

Even if your teacher understands what you're talking about, explaining the answer will take her all break by which time the Second Law will have made sure that her tea is colder than a shivering Siberian snowman. But you could be in hot water!

HOW A FRIDGE WORKS

Fridge tubes contain a chemical that turns into a gas in the part of the tube that's inside the fridge. For this to happen the chemical needs heat energy so it sucks heat from the inside of the fridge.

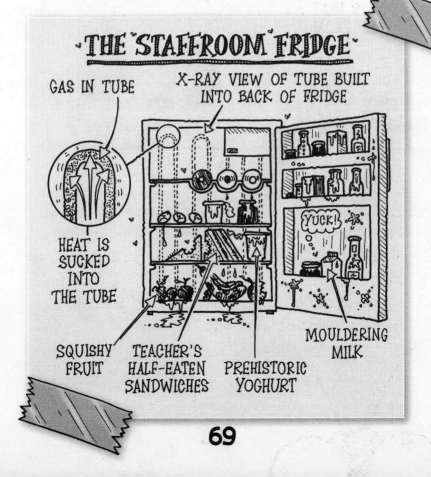

THE STAFFROOM FRIDGE

GAS IN TUBE

X-RAY VIEW OF TUBE BUILT INTO BACK OF FRIDGE

HEAT IS SUCKED INTO THE TUBE

YUCK!

SQUISHY FRUIT

TEACHER'S HALF-EATEN SANDWICHES

PREHISTORIC YOGHURT

MOULDERING MILK

In fact, fridges actually heat things up more than they cool things down! The gas is squashed into the tubes at the back of the fridge by a pump and this makes it form a liquid and release the heat energy it took from inside the fridge. And if you count the heat given out by the pump motor, fridges actually produce MORE heat than they ever suck out of your ice cream.

BET YOU NEVER KNEW!

Ice is noisy – and I don't mean when you crunch it in your mouth. Water movements under ice in the Arctic and Antarctic Oceans can put the ice under strain. This results in loss of energy in the form of sound (and a tiny amount of heat). Explorers report hearing noises like grunts, squeaks, groans, the sound of birds singing and kettles boiling. One witness said the sounds reminded him of a banjo playing...

TWANG! TWANG! TWANG!

BRAVO! ENCORE!

Of course there's loads more to find out about life in the cold, and who better to discover this than ace reporter Harvey Tucker? After his embarrassing failure with the cryogenics company Harvey's been packed off in disgrace to the Arctic to report on a polar survival course run by famous explorer Fergus Fearless...

HARVEY TUCKER'S BIG ADVENTURE

I told her I can't stand the cold!
Adventure - my bum!
I was stranded hundreds of miles from a decent bar. I was cold, I was hungry...

SHIVER!

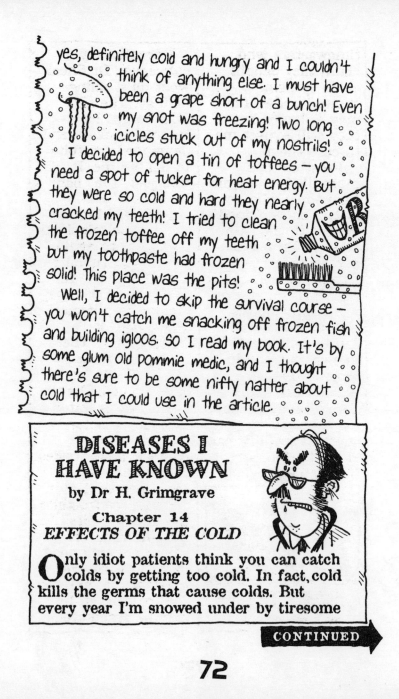

yes, definitely cold and hungry and I couldn't think of anything else. I must have been a grape short of a bunch! Even my snot was freezing! Two long icicles stuck out of my nostrils!

I decided to open a tin of toffees — you need a spot of tucker for heat energy. But they were so cold and hard they nearly cracked my teeth! I tried to clean the frozen toffee off my teeth but my toothpaste had frozen solid! This place was the pits!

Well, I decided to skip the survival course — you won't catch me snacking off frozen fish and building igloos. So I read my book. It's by some glum old pommie medic, and I thought there's sure to be some nifty natter about cold that I could use in the article.

DISEASES I HAVE KNOWN

by Dr H. Grimgrave

Chapter 14
EFFECTS OF THE COLD

Only idiot patients think you can catch colds by getting too cold. In fact, cold kills the germs that cause colds. But every year I'm snowed under by tiresome

CONTINUED ➤

timewasters who claim they caught colds by being snowed under. I'm only a doctor but they still expect me to cure them!

Frostbite is a more likely outcome for people who get lost in snow. Blood vessels in the skin close to keep heat energy in the body. The nerve endings that feel things stop working, which is why extreme cold causes numbness: it's known as frostnip. Oxygen doesn't reach these areas and, of course, they begin to die. In severe cases this can cause blisters and blackening.

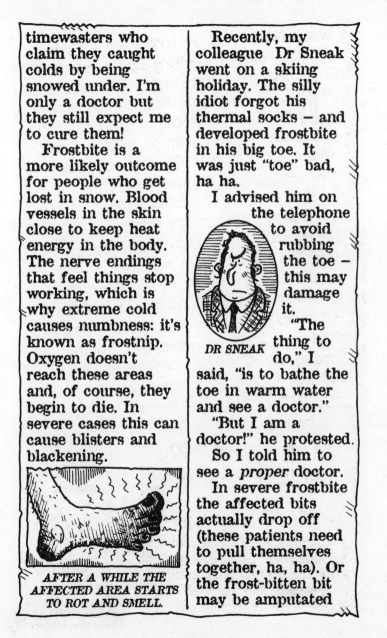

AFTER A WHILE THE AFFECTED AREA STARTS TO ROT AND SMELL.

Recently, my colleague Dr Sneak went on a skiing holiday. The silly idiot forgot his thermal socks – and developed frostbite in his big toe. It was just "toe" bad, ha ha.

I advised him on the telephone to avoid rubbing the toe – this may damage it.

DR SNEAK

"The thing to do," I said, "is to bathe the toe in warm water and see a doctor."

"But I am a doctor!" he protested.

So I told him to see a *proper* doctor.

In severe frostbite the affected bits actually drop off (these patients need to pull themselves together, ha, ha). Or the frost-bitten bit may be amputated

73

(or "chopped off" as vulgar persons say). Any readers who have lost fingers and toes would be welcome to donate them to my private medical collection. I might pay a small fee just so long as it doesn't cost an arm and a leg.

More lethal than frostbite is cooling of the body (hypothermia [hi-po-ther-me-a] as we doctors term it). Of course, every winter I get an avalanche of malingerers who think feeling a bit chilly is going to kill them – no such luck I'm afraid! I'm always cool to them. Drink hot drinks and wrap up warm – that's my advice. Physical exercise helps – I always order a five mile run for children who complain of the cold. They generally stop snivelling after the first four miles!

Real hypothermia is likely to affect idiots who go out in the cold without warm clothing and they deserve everything they get. As their bodies cool they shiver violently. They think they're hot and feel like removing clothing.

TYPICAL IDIOT

As the brain cools it sees things. One idiot even rang me and said he thought he was a pack of cards! I told him I'd deal with him later. People suffering from hypothermia need to be warmed up slowly to avoid further damage to the body. But of course what they really deserve is a good roasting!

74

Well, cop that! Reading about hypo-what's-it gave me the shivers - AH NO! shivering's a sign of hypo-thingie! I snuggled in my sleeping bag and felt hot - isn't that hypo too? I decided to build my strength by eating a mega-de-luxe family-sized pizza but it had frozen rock-solid! The cold crept up on me until it seemed to chill the marrow of my bones. I wrote my farewell letters - goodbye cruel world! But then...

"Hold on!" I thought, "Fergus Fearless might have a web-site to tell me how to stay alive - it's worth a bo-peep."

FERGUS FEARLESS TELLS YOU
HOW TO SURVIVE IN
THE ARCTIC

BEWARE FROSTBITE If you can't touch your thumb with your index finger you're in trouble - that's why this gesture traditionally means "I'm OK". Try putting your hands in your armpits to warm them up. Stamp your feet and put your feet on the tummy or in the armpits of an understanding friend.

THE TOILET Unless there's a blizzard it's safe to go outside because the vital bits are well supplied with heat energy in the form of warm blood, so they don't get frostbite as quickly as fingers and toes. WARNING: hungry husky dogs and polar bears sometimes attack explorers when they're on the toilet.

WEE!

H-E-L-P! As soon as I read these words I needed the dunny! But, oh no, it was too dangerous! This place had got on my quince! So I got on my radio blower for help. And whilst I was waiting to be rescued, I crunched my way through the rest of the frozen toffees. It seemed a shame to waste 'em!

BET YOU NEVER KNEW!

1 Frostbite was a killer condition for early explorers who were trying to reach the North and South Poles. One day American Robert Peary (1856–1920) took off his boots and eight of his toes fell off. He later remarked:

A FEW TOES WERE NOT MUCH TO GIVE TO ACHIEVE THE POLE

Do you agree?

2 In 2000 a museum received an unusual donation. Major Michael Lane sent them five of his own fingers

and eight of his toes. They had been lost to frostbite when he was climbing Mount Everest in 1976. "I don't think it was quite what they were expecting," remarked the gallant mountaineer.

3 In 1991 frostbite claimed both the hands of heroic Korean climber Kim Hong Bin on Mount McKinley, USA – but he made it to the top using his legs and teeth.

So you've read this chapter and you're an expert in dealing with deadly lack of heat energy (or "cold" as non-scientists say)? But before you move on to the next chapter, why not try your hand at this killer quiz? Could you survive the ultimate challenge and reach the North or South Pole?

COULD YOU BE A POLAR EXPLORER?

1 It's so cold that your breath has frozen and covered the inside of your hut with ice. What do you do?
a) Put up with it.
b) Melt the ice with a blow-torch.
c) Open a window.

2 Which food would give you the most energy?
a) Chocolate.
b) Spinach.
c) Greasy lumps of fat from a dead animal mixed with toffee and banana breakfast cereal.

3 You're starving hungry but you have no food left. You need food to keep warm — what do you eat first?
a) Your traditional Eskimo-style socks.
b) Your dogs.
c) Your little brother/sister.

4 When travelling to the South Pole what's the best place to store fuel for heat and cooking?
a) In blocks of ice.
b) In jars sealed with corks.
c) In jars with leather seals.

ANSWERS

1 a) It's all you can do. b) would
use up vital fuel and may set fire
to your hut and c) would make it
colder.

2 c) When explorers Dave Mitchell
and Stephen Martin walked to the
North Pole in 1994 they actually ate
this. The fat, or suet as it's
called, gives you more energy for
its weight than most other foods.
Fancy a munch?

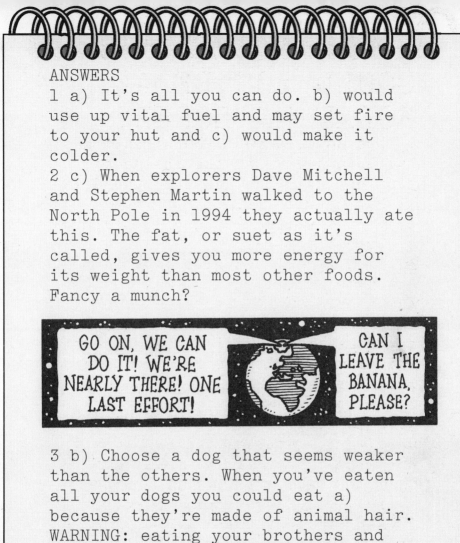

3 b) Choose a dog that seems weaker
than the others. When you've eaten
all your dogs you could eat a)
because they're made of animal hair.
WARNING: eating your brothers and
sisters is cruel and may result in a
long prison sentence.

4 b) Using ice to store fuel is
really fuel-ish … er … foolish

because you'll need fuel to make a
fire to melt the ice to get at the
fuel. In 1911 a British expedition
led by Robert Falcon Scott (1868–
1912) used c), and a rival team led
by Norwegian Roald Amundsen (1872–
1928) used b). Amundsen got to the
South Pole first. Scott's leather
seals froze and dropped off and the
Brits ran out of fuel and died of
cold. Their frozen bodies still lie
in Antarctica where they perished.

The unlucky explorers were killed by the killer science of fuel and lack of heat energy. As any scientist will tell you, fuel is a form of stored energy and, by some power-fuel coincidence, the next chapter will have you firing on all cylinders… It really is a gas!

HORRIBLY POWERFUL FUEL

Without fuel – or the energy stored in fuel – the world would grind to a chilly halt. Fuels like gas, oil, coal and petrol store the vital energy that keeps you warm and cooks your supper…

GOOD OLD FUEL!

…and fuel may well get you to school on time…

HORRIBLE FUEL!

TROUBLE IN STORE

But fuels are just one way in which energy can be stored. Here are some other ways to store energy which are just about to cause disaster for the world's most accident-prone teacher.

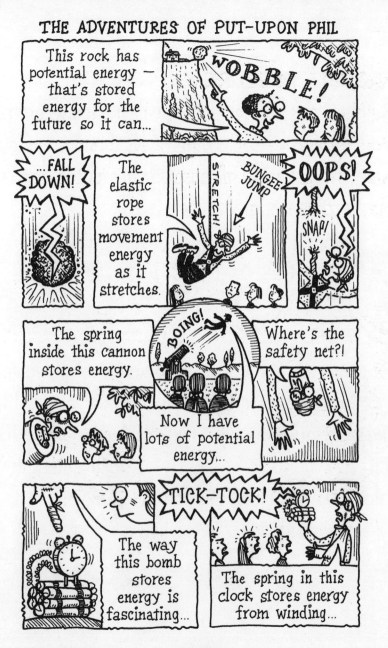

THE FUEL FACTS

For thousands of years the only fuel for most people was wood to burn in fires. Open fires provided light and heat to roast a juicy hunk of dead mammoth. But around 3000 BC an Egyptian invented the candle. No one knows this person's name but it was a *flaming* good idea – here's how it worked.

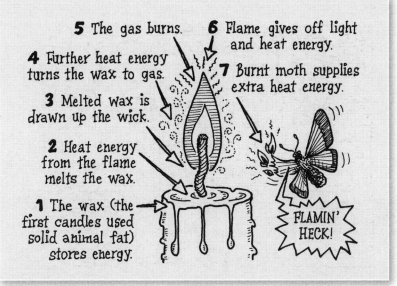

5 The gas burns.

6 Flame gives off light and heat energy.

4 Further heat energy turns the wax to gas.

7 Burnt moth supplies extra heat energy.

3 Melted wax is drawn up the wick.

2 Heat energy from the flame melts the wax.

1 The wax (the first candles used solid animal fat) stores energy.

FLAMIN' HECK!

Now the great thing about candles is that you can move them around, so they were really useful to take with you to bed if you were scared of the dark in the days before electricity. But you still need to make a flame to light the candle. Traditionally, people struck pieces of metal and flint to make sparks, but what was needed was a striking new idea…

In the 1850s Swedish inventor John Lundström invented the matches still used today. The energy is stored in the side of the box in the form of phosphorus (fos-for-rus). This substance burns when heated by the energy of the match striking the side. (If the match doesn't light it's probably on strike, ha ha.)

Anyway, phosphorus was discovered in 1669 in a revolting fashion. This story may shed some light on the subject.

A GLOW IN THE DARK

Hamburg, Germany 1677

"Yes, Herr Obermeyer, I'll tell you everything. Since you're the Mayor perhaps you can right this wrong."

And with these words, the old woman settled herself on a stool by the Mayor's fireplace and began her story.

"Sir, I'll be honest. My master, Hennig Brand, is not a good man. He is rude to us servants and grovels to people richer than himself. He married his first wife for her money, and by the time she'd died he'd spent it on science experiments. Aye, I'm not one to gossip but it's said he married the present Frau Brand for her money too. He's always trying to make gold from cheap metals. What's that? He's an alchemist? Why yes, that's what he calls himself…

"One dark evening I was passing my master's laboratory. I was taking a clean suit to his room – oh dear, what a mess my master makes of his clothes with all those chemicals! And the smells from that room are better left imagined! He had buckets of – how can I put it politely? It was wee – rotting in some experiment."

The old woman screwed up her face in disgust.

"Of course we servants weren't allowed to clean in there, but the stink was horrible enough!

Then I heard his voice. Thinking he was calling me, I crept to the door. But my master was talking to himself…

"'It glows!' I heard him say 'It's the secret of how to make gold and I've found it in wee!'

"I peered into the room. It was dark but I could see his fat excited face in a strange light that came from a glowing flask. Then he saw me and in a second he had me by the throat. He slapped my face once, twice – for all his fat he's a big strong man. He told me that he'd do terrible things if I dared to tell anyone what I'd seen.

I promised I wouldn't – I had to didn't I?

"And true to my word I've kept his secret for six years. I always think that a good servant sees everything and says nothing. And all that time my master tried to make gold from the substance. He tried and failed and tried and failed until he had spent all his wife's money.

"We began to be pestered by alchemists who wanted the secret of the glowing substance. How they heard of it I can't say – but my master had taken to boasting of his discovery in taverns. And to think – he had sworn *me* to silence!"

There was a crack, and shower of sparks leapt up the chimney from a log on the fire. The woman gave a little gasp and looked up in alarm as if expecting to see her master's angry face. Then she continued her story.

"One night my master was visited by a Herr Krafft. He offered to give my master money in return for the secret. But my master was sly as well as greedy. He wouldn't tell Herr Krafft how he made the glowing material but he promised to sell what he had. He added with a low laugh that he could make plenty more.

"I wanted to tell Herr Krafft that the substance was made of wee but I was afraid of my master's temper. So I sat quietly with my sewing. Suddenly there was a pounding on the door.

"It was Herr Kunckel, he was an alchemist who had called to see the strange substance a few days before. Herr Kunckel also wanted to buy some of the chemical but my master told him rudely that he'd failed to make any more. I heard my master whisper, 'yes, it's made of wee, now go away!'

"Then, looking flustered, he came back and closed his deal with Herr Krafft.

"After Herr Krafft left, my master began to dance. Soon he was slapping his legs and laughing fit to burst.

"His friend the innkeeper came round and my master ordered me to fetch wine. After a bottle or two my master was drunk. His fat face shone red and shiny in the firelight and his voice was loud and slurred as he boasted of how he had tricked Herr Krafft and Herr Kunckel.

"The innkeeper leaned forward and prodded my master's belly.

"'So what's this substance made of – you old crook?'

"My master exploded with laughter until his chins wobbled.

"'Wee' he snorted, 'left to rot and heated until it's just a white powder at the bottom of a flask – then heated again! Two hundred thalers – just think of it – two hundred silver thalers for a pot of wee!'

"My master laughed until he rocked backwards and forwards. Then he wiped his wet lips and clumsily tapped his nose.

"'Remember, old friend, not a word of this.' he hissed.

"Well, sir, I am sure you've heard what happened next – it was the talk of Hamburg. Herr Kunckel made his own glowing substance. And they do say that Herr Krafft made a fortune showing it to kings and queens all over Europe. And now Kunckel and Krafft are telling everyone that *they* discovered the chemical! My master was in a foul mood for days – he's been unbearable! And that's why I am here to testify that my master, Hennig Brand, made the discovery first.

"A good servant never offers an opinion but I must add a word of my own. Sir, I wish this substance had never been found! It's like an evil genie making men cruel and selfish and greedy so that they trick one another and tell lies. What's that? How can I prove what I say is true?"

The woman looked troubled.

"I'm only a poor serving woman – I have only my word – and this…"

She opened her bag and slowly drew out a small flask. The flask contained a powder that shone with the ghostly glow of green fire.

BET YOU NEVER KNEW!

1 When phosphorous atoms combine with oxygen in the air, the atoms give out their stored energy in the form of light. Although phosphorus is poisonous it was made into pills to cure stomach and lung diseases. The pills were useless and the people who ate them felt sick and began to glow in the dark.

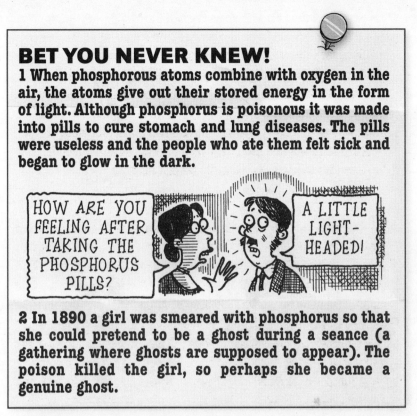

HOW ARE YOU FEELING AFTER TAKING THE PHOSPHORUS PILLS?

A LITTLE LIGHT-HEADED!

2 In 1890 a girl was smeared with phosphorus so that she could pretend to be a ghost during a seance (a gathering where ghosts are supposed to appear). The poison killed the girl, so perhaps she became a genuine ghost.

Today few Europeans and Americans use candles and open fires. (Mind you, it's rumoured that in power cuts mean-spirited teachers wrap themselves in woolly scarves and teach by the light of candles. Anything to avoid sending their pupils home.)

But mostly we rely on gas or electricity produced from coal, gas or oil. Now I expect you're keen to find out about these vital forms of energy, so we've invited an expert to answer your questions…

HORRIBLE SCIENCE QUESTION TIME
With Bernard Boyle of the Energy Department

I'm here to explain about fuel.

FUEL

You're here to give us the fuel facts?

Yes, I won't leave anything out.

A hundred years ago the main type of fuel was coal. This is a fossil fuel…

What's a fossil fuel?

KILLER EXPRESSIONS...

Do you say...

I'M A RHINO-ANALYST...

AND I'M AN EXPERT STENCHER

WOW! I LIKE RHINOS TOO BUT YOUR FRIEND SOUNDS A REAL STINKER!

ANSWER

DON'T YOU DARE!!! The killer scientists might attack you! A rhino-analyst studies smells in cooking gas. The actual gas doesn't smell, so smelly sulphur chemicals are added to the gas to make it pong so that people notice if they leave their gas taps on – this is called "stenching".

Although gas is often removed from rocks where there's oil, a cooking and lighting gas can also be made from coal. And I bet you never knew that this fact was discovered by a ingenious inventor with a terrible taste in hats...

Hall of Fame: William Murdock (1754–1839)
Nationality: Scottish

Mrs Murdock was furious...

"Ye greet daftie – luik wat ye've done to ma best china tea pot! It's ruined – ye greet muckle lump! It's nay guid noo! Ye've nay sense – tho ye be ma ane laddie! (Mrs Murdock probably used other words that were too rude to repeat in a respectable book like this.)

Young William bowed his head and was just mumbling something about science experiments when the tea pot whizzed past his ear and smashed to pieces on the black iron stove behind him.

But he had actually made a vital discovery. By heating coal (yes, in his mum's tea pot) he had found out that you can make a gas that burns to produce heat and light energy. But then William always was a practical lad. Already he had built his own tricycle out of wood to get to school on time. This was surprising because:

1 He was keen to get to school.

2 The bicycle hadn't been invented yet!

When William was 23, he heard about a factory in England where they made the most powerful steam engines in the whole world. He was so excited that he *walked* hundreds of kilometres to the Soho Works in Birmingham to ask for a job. The boss, Matthew Boulton, was about to show William the door when the young man's hat fell off. It hit the floor with a solid clunk, as well it might since it was made of wood. Yes, the hat was one of William's inventions and it proved the lad was no wooden head.

For the rest of his life William worked for Matthew Boulton and his partner, Scottish steam-engine inventor James Watt (1736–1819). He repaired steam engines all over the country but still found time to invent a steam-powered carriage and a method of using fish skin to remove cloudiness from beer (if your dad's into home brew this could spell doom for your pet goldfish).

William developed his coal gas idea. He began by heating coal in a tank and pumping it round pipes where the gas could be lit from special gas taps.

First William lit the cottage in Cornwall where he was working and then the Soho works. Boulton was delighted by the discovery but he stopped William patenting his idea. Eventually other people copied him and he made no money from it.

THE FUEL CRISIS STARTS TO BITE

Remember what Bernard Boyle was saying about fossil fuels running out? You may have heard people talking about it. There's enough coal underground to keep us warm and cosy until about 2160 but oil and gas won't last that long – especially if the world can't learn to use less of them. No wonder some scientists think we need a new kind of energy – and they're prepared to think very, very small…

Killer energy fact file

Name: Nuclear power

Basic facts:

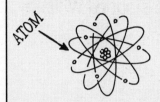
ATOM

1 Remember the atoms on page 39? Here's a quick reminder if you don't...

Atoms are held together by enormous forces. But this means that if the atoms are torn apart the energy of these forces are released, together with deadly high-energy radioactive rays that can kill by blistering the skin and destroying the lining of the guts.

2 One kg of uranium atoms produces enough energy to lift 200 million elephants one metre in the air.

3 In nuclear power stations the heat energy made by splitting atoms boils water to steam that drives turbines and makes electricity.

Killer details:

1 Nuclear power stations can suffer terrible accidents. At Chernobyl, Ukraine in 1986 and Fukushima, Japan in 2011 deadly radioactive pollution escaped from damaged power stations.

2 The power stations create radioactive waste that can stay dangerous for tens of thousands of years.

SPOT THE POWER QUIZ

Some unusual materials have been used to make power. Have you the brain-power to spot the fuel that no one's ever tried?
1 Dead cows
2 Waste cooking oil from chip shops
3 Smelly rotten eggs
4 Used nappies

ANSWER
3 But who "nose" what might happen in the future?

As for the others, in 2000...
1 Some English power stations were making electricity from burning the remains of diseased cows. I suppose that's what they call moo-clear energy.
2 A man in Manchester, England ran his car on oil from his local chip shop that had been changed chemically into diesel oil. I suppose he could have run it on

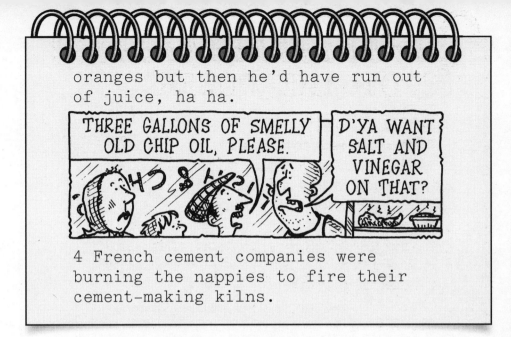

oranges but then he'd have run out of juice, ha ha.

> THREE GALLONS OF SMELLY OLD CHIP OIL, PLEASE.

> D'YA WANT SALT AND VINEGAR ON THAT?

4 French cement companies were burning the nappies to fire their cement-making kilns.

You can also make power from wind, waves, tides and solar power (that's the heat and light of the sun). These natural types of energy are called "renewable" because there's always more of them being made. And deep within the Earth there's another type of renewable energy: here's how YOU can tap into it…

HOW TO BUILD YOUR OWN
GEOTHERMAL POWER STATION

INTRODUCTION

Geothermal power uses the mass of molten rock thousands of metres under your feet to make heat energy. This power actually makes it possible to grow bananas in Iceland (in heated greenhouses)

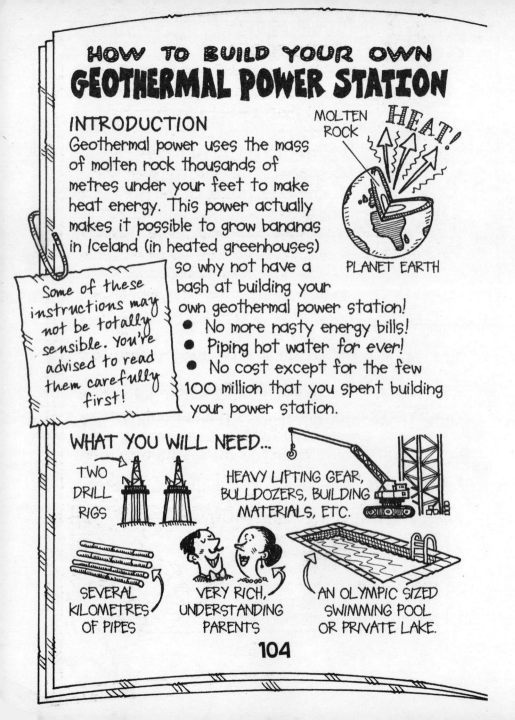

MOLTEN ROCK

HEAT!

PLANET EARTH

so why not have a bash at building your own geothermal power station!

Some of these instructions may not be totally sensible. You're advised to read them carefully first!

- No more nasty energy bills!
- Piping hot water for ever!
- No cost except for the few 100 million that you spent building your power station.

WHAT YOU WILL NEED...

TWO DRILL RIGS

HEAVY LIFTING GEAR, BULLDOZERS, BUILDING MATERIALS, ETC.

SEVERAL KILOMETRES OF PIPES

VERY RICH, UNDERSTANDING PARENTS

AN OLYMPIC SIZED SWIMMING POOL OR PRIVATE LAKE.

HOT ROCKS

INSTRUCTIONS

1. Set up your drill rigs and drill 7 km down until you reach some rocks that are hot enough to boil water.

2. Don't forget to push down the pipes into the holes after your drills.

HOUSE

PIPES

3. Remember to link up the pipes from your second bore hole with the hot water system of your house. I expect your friend's parents will be delighted to have their homes plumbed in too!

POOL

4. Now for the FUN bit! Link up the pipes to your first rig to the swimming pool and turn on the taps so the water rushes down into the first bore hole.

BOILING WATER

5. Superheated hot water will rush up the second bore hole and into your hot water system! Warning: you might need to adjust the pressure or your radiators may explode!

THE SMALL PRINT

If molten rock oozes from your bore holes you've created a volcano that could bury your neighbourhood and school under thousands of tonnes of red hot lava. This may be a good moment to leave the country.

WHOOPS!

And if you're cold you can rub your hands together. Remember how the drilled cannon made heat on page 41? Yes, that's right – in the same way, your hands rub together and the rubbing force (known as friction) turns movement energy into heat energy – easy-peasy!

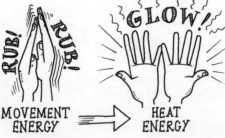

MOVEMENT ENERGY ⟹ HEAT ENERGY

Mind you, you'll find plenty of movement energy in the next chapter. In fact, it's just about to move off *now*!

THE POWER TO MOVE YOU

Look out the window and you're sure to see something moving. You might see a cat chasing a mouse, or a dog chasing the cat, or children chasing the dog … or the neighbours chasing the children or maybe everyone being chased by a killer Tyrannosaurus.

Well, they've all got something in common and it's called…

KILLER EXPRESSIONS

Do you say...

I STUDY KINETIC ENERGY

MY CAT'S GOT LOADS OF KITTY ENERGY!

ANSWER

Don't show off the paw state of your knowledge. Kinetic (ki-net-tic) energy is the scientific name for movement energy. That's right — every move you make is powered by kinetic energy.

BET YOU NEVER KNEW!

Any kind of kinetic energy loses heat energy. If you don't believe me, try going for a run...

SPOT THE DIFFERENCE

BEFORE — GOING FOR A RUN

AFTER — GLOWING FROM A RUN

Machines also lose loads of heat, as you'll discover on page 125.

Kinetic energy moves caterpillars and cars and comets and ... well, everything, really. It even powers monster waves known as mega-tsunami (meg-a-tu-nar-me). Vast landslides into the sea provide kinetic energy for killer waves. They sweep across the ocean and arrive at the opposite shore half a kilometre high! But DON'T PANIC! Waves this big happen once in tens of thousands of years. Anyway, here's how to make your own model mega-tsunami ... without wrecking your house too badly.

DARE YOU DISCOVER ... HOW MOVEMENT ENERGY WORKS?

You will need:

A TORCH

A WASHING UP BOWL OF WATER
(IDEALLY THIS SHOULD BE PLACED IN
THE KITCHEN SINK AND NOT OVER
YOUR BROTHER/SISTER'S HEAD.)

What you do:

1 Wait until it's dark. Switch on the torch and hold it about 60 cm above the bowl.

2 Set the mixer tap so that a drop of water falls into the basin. (Or you could pick up a drop on your finger and let it fall from about 30 cm into the bowl.)

What do you notice?

a) Ripples spread out from the middle and then disappear.

b) Ripples move inwards from the side.

c) The ripples spread out to the sides and then move back.

ANSWER

c) Did you spot the faint returning ripples? The kinetic energy of the falling drop makes ripples of movement energy through the water. The ripple loses energy to the sides and this makes it appear fainter as it returns to the centre.

MAGIC MACHINES

The idea behind many hand-operated machines is to make life a bit easier by saving us energy. For example, using a tin-opener uses less energy than the alternative…

But many machines need even less human energy. These are machines that are powered by fuel energy, and right now it's time to meet the grand-daddy of all these types of machine…

This idea might have set Roman technology steaming ahead. Just think – the Romans might have built steam trains and steam ships ... but they didn't. As the magazine said, no one knew what to do with steam engines and the Romans weren't that bothered about saving muscle energy. Not whilst they had lots of slaves to do all the hard work.

It took another 1,600 years for an inventor named Thomas Savery (1650–1715) to reinvent the idea. One evening he drank a bottle of wine. He was too drunk to throw the bottle away – so he chucked it on the fire. Steam puffed from the bottle and Savery was just sober enough to see that the remaining wine was turning to steam. So the boozy boffin pulled the bottle from the fire and stuck it in water to cool it down and then, to his amazement, the water was sucked into the bottle!

But what was going on?

COULD YOU BE A SCIENTIST?

So what do you think was causing this effect?

a) As the bottle cooled it grew slightly larger and this made room for the water.

b) As the air cooled it took up less space so the water flooded in.

c) The hot wine was pulling in the water by a mysterious force.

ANSWER

b) When air has heat energy it pushes outwards, remember? As the air cools it takes up less space.

Savery worked this out and designed engines for pumping water from mines. Over the next 80 years inventors like Thomas Newcomen (1663–1729) and James Watt improved the steam engine until it could power any kind of machinery, and transport like trains and ships. The world was transformed, and all because a tipsy scientist had a lot of bottle.

Here's one of Watt's inventions – Watt an invention, eh? It's a wonderful way to turn heat energy into movement energy (that's the First Law of Thermodynamics from page 19).

A FEW FACTS TO GET STEAMED UP ABOUT...

1 Inventors were fascinated by steam engines. In the 1730s an 11-year-old boy named John Smeaton (1724–1792) was taken to see one of Newcomen's machines. He was so excited he built a model steam engine and used it to pump out his dad's goldfish pond. Don't try this at home!

You'll be pleased to know that John survived the punishment he got from his dad and grew up to be a famous engineer who built canals and lighthouses.

2 Inventors like William Murdock built steam carriages that ran on the road like cars today. In 1801 Murdock's pal, inventor Richard Trevithick (1771–1833), built his own steam carriage and took it for a spin. It broke down, but the inventor managed to fix it and went to the pub to celebrate.

Unfortunately he left the fire on – the boiler boiled dry and the engine exploded. That must have been a BLASTED nuisance!

3 In 1894 inventor Hiram Maxim (1840–1916) built a giant plane with wings 34 metres across powered by steam engines. The engines weren't powerful enough to get the heavy plane flying. The plane managed to get a few centimetres into the air before crashing into a crumpled wreck. I expect Maxim got a bit steamed up about the accident.

But the most successful use for steam power turned out to be the steam turbine. As you discovered on page 94 – turbines are used to make electricity in power stations. But that proved to be the least of their uses – as you're about to find out…

Hall of Fame: Charles Parsons (1854–1931)
Nationality: Irish

Young Charles was born with a silver spoon in his mouth. NO, he didn't get a valuable bit of cutlery stuck in his gob! He was born filthy rich. His dad was a science-mad astronomer who happened to be the Earl of Rosse and owned his own castle. In 1845 the Earl built the world's largest telescope — at an astronomical cost. But the 15-metre monster proved a real big mistake since you could only use it when the sky was clear and in that part of Ireland it was usually raining.

Young Charles was too rich to go to school — so like James Joule he had his own personal teacher. Charles became interested in science and began to invent machines. He built a steam-powered carriage and gave his brothers rides. One day he took his aunt for a ride but she fell off the machine and died.

I BET YOU'RE **DEAD** IMPRESSED! I'VE BEEN **DYING** TO SHOW IT TO YOU!

Charles joined a company that built steam engines. He enjoyed his work so much that when he got married his idea of a romantic honeymoon was dragging his bride off to watch the testing of his newly invented turbines on a miserably cold lake. Charles came away with a lot of scientific data and his wife came away with a nasty dose of fever.

In the 1880s Charles developed his idea for the turbine. The idea was very simple: hot steam energy powered small turning blades. In fact, the blades turned very fast and Charles realized that they could be used to turn a propeller and power a ship. Here's what happened next...

The secret diary of Rear-Admiral Lord Blewitt

1894 ~ I've just had a visit from that inventor chappie Parsons. Perfect crack-pot, just like his father! I've never heard such piffle and humbug! He says he can build a ship that sails at 34 knots - that's faster than any ship afloat! Parsons says he's got a working model but I told him in no uncertain terms that nothing is faster than an ordinary steam engine. Personally, though, I can't see what's wrong with wind-power - it was good enough when I was a boy!

1895 ~ Yet another letter from that blasted nuisance Parsons. He's been pestering my fellow admirals with his half-cracked ideas. Can't he take NO for an answer? That fellow should be keel-hauled and flogged with the cat! His letter is full of scientific balderdash. He says he's built an actual boat now and he wants to show it off to us.
That's out of the question!!! We admirals have more important things to do - like going for cruises!

1896 - Please excuse the shaky writing - I am in a state of shock. Today was Fleet Review Day. Every year we admirals watch proudly as our great fleet steams past and raise a glass of port to Her Majesty's good health! But not today. Oh no...

Blow me if the whole proceedings weren't completely ruined by a little boat dashing past at 34 knots! I was so taken aback I began to splutter and my false teeth fell out! Poor old Admiral Snuff was so upset he spent the whole day peering through the wrong end of his telescope!

I took a look through my own glass and saw that confounded blighter Parsons on the fast boat. He was actually grinning and waving! If I'd had my way our warships would have blown him out of the water! But, er ... no one could catch him, actually! I'm afraid he left even our fastest ships astern.

My fellow admirals are talking about ordering these new-fangled turbines. It seems that our entire navy has just become out of date! I have a real sinking feeling about all this...

123

You'll be pleased to know that Parsons became rich and famous although he later wasted most of his money trying to make diamonds out of graphite – that's the substance used to make pencil lead. Oh well, no doubt he thought he was on the write lines.

THE ULTIMATE FREEBIE

Mind you, for hundreds of years scientists having been trying to build an even more powerful machine. A machine that *never* needs any new energy! A machine that once it starts will never, ever stop! I suppose that's what our hungry reporter pal Harvey Tucker would call "the ultimate free lunch". Scientists call it "perpetual motion".

BUT HOLD ON, DIDN'T YOU SAY ON PAGE 20 THAT THE SECOND LAW SAYS THAT EVERYTHING LOSES ENERGY IN THE FORM OF HEAT AND THAT MEANS YOU HAVE TO KEEP PUTTING MORE ENERGY INTO IT?

A VERY ALERT READER

Hey, that's right! And what's more, as I said earlier, movement energy leads to a loss of heat energy and this means that sooner or later any machine will always run out of energy. In 1824 French scientist Nicolas Carnot (1796–1832) worked out that steam engines will never work perfectly for this reason. But I didn't say that perpetual motion worked, did I? Mind you, it took a while for scientists to figure this out…

THE SCIENTIST'S FRIEND

Problem Page with Professor Frank Helper

Are you a scientist with an embarrassing problem? Do you feel it would help to talk to someone who cares? If so write to me and no one need know your secret except, of course, our 567,000 readers! This week – perpetual motion...

Dear Frank,
I've built this perpetual motion machine but it doesn't work. It's a bit worrying, me being a famous architect and all that. Am I a bit of a plonker?
Villard de Honnecourt
(14th century)

Dear Villard,
You certainly are! Your wheel will always stop owing to friction between the wheel and axle which turns the movement energy of the wheel into heat energy. Perhaps you ought to throw your energy into architecture?

Dear Frank,
I'm a science-mad nobleman. I'm also a big supporter of King Charles in his battles with Parliament and I've been arrested and imprisoned a few times – but that's enough about me. Anyway, I've built this perpetual motion wheel operated by falling balls – see my drawing. It spins for ages but

CONTINUED ➜

126

then it stops. Why? Why? My head is spinning faster than my wheel — help me!
Yours nobly,
Edward Somerset
The 2nd Marquis
of Worcester (1601-1667)

Dear Marquis
The falling balls have no effect on your lordship's wheel. The wheel — er, I mean real — reason it stops is friction. See my answer to Villard.

Dear Frank,
I've gotta this bellissima perpetual motion machine! It's powered by de wind power and it's perfectissimo except for one tiny detail - it wonna work! I'd be humbly grateful for ever for ☺ ☺ your most kind advice.

Marco Zimara (Italy 1500s)

TURNING SAIL SQUEEZES DE BELLOWS TO MAKE MORE OF DE WIND.

WIND BLOWS THE SAILS ROUND

Dear Marco,
My most kind advice is, forget it! Your machine is a load of hot air! The sails lose energy from friction and don't have enough energy to squeeze the bellows. So I'm afraid you're out of puff, pal.

Yes, perpetual motion is about as likely as a puppy dog that doesn't pee in your slippers. Italian mega-genius Leonardo da Vinci (1452–1519) put it a bit more elegantly:

Oh you students of eternal motion! How many futile things have you created while searching for it.

And old Leo ought to know – he built his own machine which (please don't faint with surprise) didn't work.

Italian scientist Gerolamo Cardano (1501–1576) used maths to figure out that perpetual motion was impossible. Gerolamo led an exciting life. He was brought up by his strict grandmother who was cruel to him when he was naughty. (I hope your granny is a bit less vicious!) Gerolamo became a doctor and a scientist who claimed (rightly) that fire isn't a substance as people thought at the time, but then he found himself facing a fearsome fiery fate…

In 1570 he was arrested by the Church for using his interest in astrology (star signs) to speculate about religion. He was threatened with torture and burning to death unless he confessed he was wrong. Should he confess? It was a burning question. Clever Cardano did the sensible thing and he was released.

But later on his son murdered someone and had his head chopped off. Gerolamo fell out with his second son and asked the government to banish him to another city as "a youth of evil habits". Hopefully your dad is a bit less strict with you!

So there you are – perpetual motion is impossible. The laws of energy just won't allow it.

But what's this?

PERPETUAL MOTION AT LAST!!!

COME AND SEE THE PERPETUAL MOTION MACHINE INVENTED BY ME, JOHANN BESSLER OTHERWISE KNOWN AS "ORFFYREUS" USING THE LATEST 1680s TECHNOLOGY.

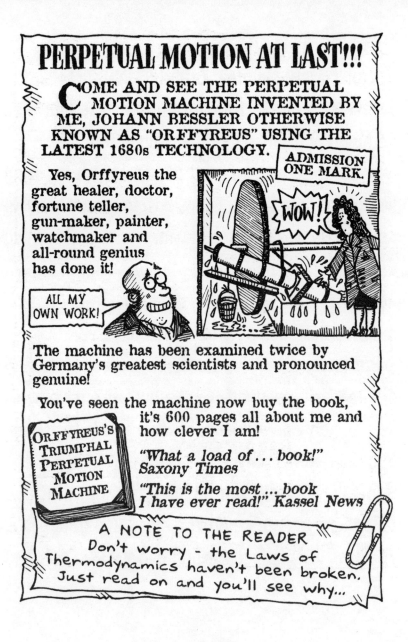

Yes, Orffyreus the great healer, doctor, fortune teller, gun-maker, painter, watchmaker and all-round genius has done it!

ADMISSION ONE MARK.

WOW!

ALL MY OWN WORK!

The machine has been examined twice by Germany's greatest scientists and pronounced genuine!

You've seen the machine now buy the book, it's 600 pages all about me and how clever I am!

ORFFYREUS'S TRIUMPHAL PERPETUAL MOTION MACHINE

"What a load of ... book!" Saxony Times

"This is the most ... book I have ever read!" Kassel News

A NOTE TO THE READER
Don't worry - the Laws of Thermodynamics haven't been broken. Just read on and you'll see why...

CONFESSION

I, Gretel Braun, the servant girl of Johann Bessler, confess that my master is a crook and his machine was built to trick foolish people out of their money. He spent his wife's savings building this machine but he wouldn't let anyone look at its insides — not even the scientists who said it was genuine. And why? Because there's a handle next door that turns the wheel! I should know — I had to crank that flipping handle every time people came to see the machine.

Ouch my poor back!

PS Please don't execute me — I was only doing my job!

Yes, Johann's machine relied on good old-fashioned muscle power. And that brings us to the next chapter. Actually I'm not going to tell you what's in it because I don't want to spoil the surprise.

But here's a hint… It's hot, it's sweaty and it's all yours…

HOT, SWEATY BODY BITS

This chapter is about how your body uses energy. Yes, this is the chapter in which the going gets tough. And you know what that means? The tough get going – and Harvey Tucker slobs out with a bucket of popcorn in front of the telly...

133

Killer energy fact file

Name: Your body and energy

Basic facts: 1 The body is a living machine for turning the stored energy in your food into movement energy to move your muscles.

2 Actually only one-quarter of the energy that your muscles use is used for movement – the rest becomes heat energy and escapes from the body.

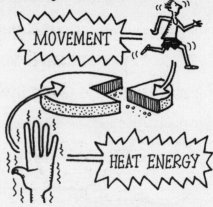

Killer details: Did you know that the energy in your body is made by tiny creatures that were once killer germs?

It's true!

Read on for more dreadful details...

WORKING UP A SWEAT

Tough exercise is all in a day's work for athletes. In 2000, marathon runner Tegla Loroupe from Kenya said she took up running because she had to walk 10 km to school and was punished if she was late. Soon she was running 192 km a week. That's like running to school and all the way home again and all the way to school a second time. And doing it all again in the afternoon. And doing this every school day.

Wanna try it?

And speaking of exercise, here's a few killer holidays Harvey Tucker wouldn't be seen dead on (well, if he tried them he might be dead on them)…

DYING FOR A DANCE?

YOU COULD BE DYING FOR EVER
AT OUR OLD-TIME 1930S
AMERICAN DANCE MARATHON.

Yes, you have to dance until you
drop - the winner is the person
who stays on their feet for longest.

RULES ~ 1. No sleeping. 2. You *must* keep moving. Anyone
not dancing fast enough gets wet towels flicked at their legs! 3.
You have 15 minutes rest in each hour - so make sure you go to the
toilet and receive life-saving medical treatment in this time.

4. If you die during the dance marathon you get
disqualified.

IMPORTANT ANNOUNCEMENT

We've just found out that
dance marathons have been
BANNED in the USA since
1937 after several people
went mad with tiredness. This
holiday has been cancelled!
Anyone who has booked will
get a full refund ... that's if
they can find where we've
hidden the money.

Mind you, in the 1940s, dance marathons continued to be held in secret…

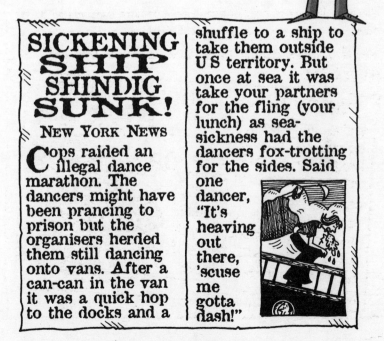

SICKENING SHIP SHINDIG SUNK!

NEW YORK NEWS

Cops raided an illegal dance marathon. The dancers might have been prancing to prison but the organisers herded them still dancing onto vans. After a can-can in the van it was a quick hop to the docks and a shuffle to a ship to take them outside U S territory. But once at sea it was take your partners for the fling (your lunch) as seasickness had the dancers fox-trotting for the sides. Said one dancer, "It's heaving out there, 'scuse me gotta dash!"

HORRIBLE SCIENCE

FITNESS HOLIDAYS

DANCE MARATHONS TOO *SOFT* FOR YOU?
WHY NOT TRY THE

WESTERN STATES ENDURANCE RUN?!

YOU'VE GOT TO RUN 161 KM (100 MILES) IN LESS THAN 30 HOURS. YOU HAVE TO RUN UP MOUNTAINS AND AVOID RATTLESNAKES.

WARNING!
YOUR BODY WILL DRY OUT IN THE HEAT AND YOU MAY LOSE 7% OF YOUR WEIGHT.

← START
FINISH →

AND WHILE YOU'RE AT IT, WHY NOT TRY THE

HAWAII IRONMAN COMPETITION?

SPLASH!
PEDAL!
STRIDE!

1 Swim	2 Cycle	3 Run a marathon
3.86 km	180 km	42.2 km
(2.4 miles)	(112 miles)	(26.2 miles)

WARNING!
WE'VE ALLOWED A DAY FOR THE *WHOLE COMPETITION* SO YOU'D BEST HURRY OR YOU'LL MISS YOUR FLIGHT AND HAVE TO SWIM HOME ACROSS THE **PACIFIC OCEAN**.

But all this energy raises a sensational scientific question – how exactly do our bodies turn stored food energy into action-packed movement energy? How can a stodgy old school dinner help you turn in a world athletic running record? (And we're not talking about getting the squirts and having to dash for the loo.)

First the theories...

1 Three hundred years ago scientists believed the muscles contained gunpowder that exploded to make them move. This idea wasn't as silly as it sounds because gunpowder is a form of stored energy and the muscles do use stored food energy (see below if you don't believe me).

2 French chemist Antoine Lavoisier (1743–1794) was interested in burning and breathing and pointed out that you breathe more when you work hard. Well, blow me if he wasn't right! Lavoisier reckoned that some kind of burning was going on in the lungs to change food into energy.

3 Then another scientist, Joseph-Louis Lagrange (1736–1813) said that if the lungs burnt food they'd catch fire. Hopefully your lungs won't do this – not even when you've eaten a really hot chilli.

4 German scientist Justus von Liebig (1803–1873) reckoned that the body's vital force moved the muscles.

But none of these clever and very thoughtful scientists grasped the truth. The answer to how the body uses energy is a small detail – how small? Oh, about 0.02 mm across. It's called a cell, and to find out more why not read this rare copy of HOW YOUR BODY WORKS by the famous Dr Jekyll and Mr Hyde. Apparently Dr Jekyll's quite nice but when he drinks a potion he turns into a blood-crazed killer monster…

HOW YOUR BODY WORKS

by Dr Jekyll and Mr Hyde

INTRODUCTION

Dr Jekyll writes... Dear Reader Welcome to our little book about how the body works. We're sure you'll enjoy reading its fascinating facts and looking at its ever so interesting diagrams...

Dr J

Mr Hyde writes... GRRR! Read on you scumbags or I'll break into your houses and rip your hearts out and eat them! Yummy - I'm feeling peckish! HA, HA, HA!

Mr H

Chapter 1: Feeding your cells

Dr Jekyll writes. . .

Your body is made up of trillions of human body cells that need energy to put together proteins. These are chemicals that build into all the useful bits that make up the body. Every cell is a teeny-weenie living machine that makes power in hundreds of tiny units called **mitochondria** (mi-toe-con-dree-a). Mitochondria make energy using glucose — it's a very tasty type of sugar found in foods such as flour, bread, cereal and sweet things like dainty little pastries...

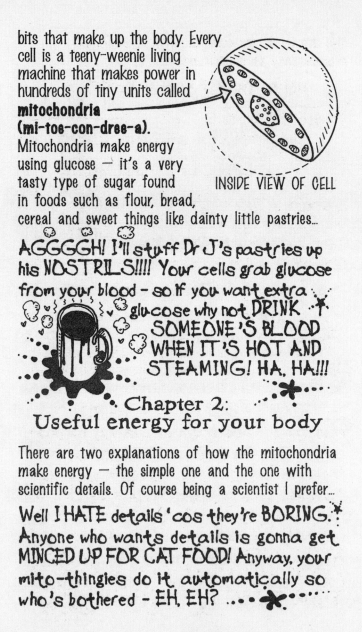

INSIDE VIEW OF CELL

AGGGGH! I'll stuff Dr J's pastries up his NOSTRILS!!!! Your cells grab glucose from your blood - so if you want extra glucose why not DRINK SOMEONE'S BLOOD WHEN IT'S HOT AND STEAMING! HA, HA!!!

Chapter 2:
Useful energy for your body

There are two explanations of how the mitochondria make energy — the simple one and the one with scientific details. Of course being a scientist I prefer...

Well I HATE details 'cos they're BORING. Anyone who wants details is gonna get MINCED UP FOR CAT FOOD! Anyway, your mito-thingies do it automatically so who's bothered - EH, EH? ....

I've drawn a nice clear diagram to make the process easy to understand.

HOW CELLS MAKE ENERGY

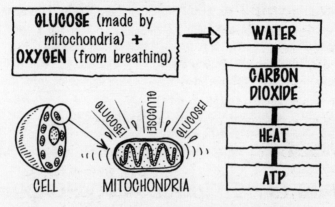

GLUCOSE (made by mitochondria) **+ OXYGEN** (from breathing) →

WATER

CARBON DIOXIDE

HEAT

ATP

CELL   MITOCHONDRIA   GLUCOSE! GLUCOSE! GLUCOSE!

ATP, or Adenosine Triphosphate (A-deen-o-sin Try-fos-fate) as we scientists call it, is a lovely little chemical energy store that goes wherever it's needed in the cell to make energy to power your muscles or make new bits of the cell...

And the old bod can make energy without oxygen, like when someone tries to run away from me. But they can't get enough oxygen to their cells and they're gasping. HA HA HA! Their stupid cells try to make energy without oxygen but can't make as much ATP and SO I GRAB THEM AND PLAY MARBLES WITH THEIR EYEBALLS! HA! HA HA!

MIGHTY MYSTERIOUS MITOCHONDRIA

1 Inside you right now are about 10,000,000,000,000,000 (ten million billion) mitochondria busily churning out energy to keep your body going. But they're so small that you can fit one billion of them inside a grain of sand.

2 Mitochondria look like very tiny brown-red worms and when they make more of themselves they spilt in half. Scientists think that mitochondria were once germs that moved into cells a billion years ago. At first they were a pest but somehow the cells and mitochondria worked out how to live together…

And now every time you eat and every time you breathe you are doing it to feed alien life-forms hiding in your body!

3 You get your mitochondria from your mum. That's because the mitochondria in your cells are descended from a tiny egg made by your mum. Actually your energy level depends on lots of things like health and diet, but basically you get your energy from your mum!

MASSIVE MUSCLES

The part of your body that *really* needs energy is your muscles. It doesn't matter whether your muscles are bulging and beefy or you look like a stick insect on a diet. Your muscles are where your body turns stored chemical energy from ATP into movement energy.

And now for some facts you can muscle into...

Killer energy fact file

Name: Muscles

Basic facts: 1 The word "muscle" means "little mouse" in Latin. The Romans thought that muscles looked like mice scampering about under the skin.

2 All muscles are made of fibres that shorten in response to nerve signals from the brain. When the fibres relax *so* does the muscle.

3 Here are the main types of muscle.

• Smooth muscles make moves you can't control like shifting the food in your guts. These muscles aren't too strong.

• Striped muscles move your body. You can control these.

Killer details: Muscles often come in pairs with opposing jobs – your biceps bends your arm and your triceps straightens it, for example. Some body builders develop such huge biceps that they can't straighten their arms properly.

So you've got your head around how your body makes energy from mitochondria to muscles? Well, that's fab! Hopefully you've still got enough energy to try this rather exhausting quiz…

SEVEN SUPER-ENERGY QUIZ QUESTIONS

You should be able to race through this quiz because each question has just TWO possible answers. I just hope you're not in two minds about it!

1 Babies are more likely to have this than adults — what is it?
a) Built-in central heating.
b) Cold blood.

2 How much heat energy does your body give off when you're watching telly for an hour?
a) As much as an electric heater.
b) As much as a light bulb.

3 Why do children seem to have more energy than adults?
a) Children make energy faster than adults.
b) People of all ages produce the same amount of energy but adults prefer slobbing about.

4 Why do some people get overweight?
a) They eat more than they should.

b) Their bodies burn up food more slowly and spare food is stored as fat.

5 Which of these statements is correct?

a) Lazy people live longer than hard-working people because they use up less energy.

b) Hard work never killed anyone (as Dr Grimgrave likes to remind us).

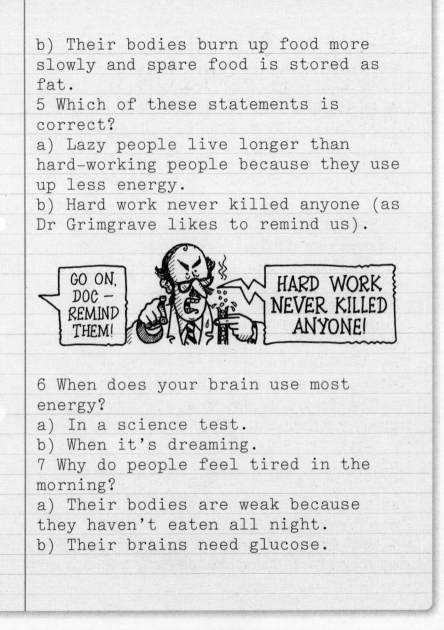

6 When does your brain use most energy?

a) In a science test.

b) When it's dreaming.

7 Why do people feel tired in the morning?

a) Their bodies are weak because they haven't eaten all night.

b) Their brains need glucose.

ANSWERS

1 a) Yes, babies really have central heating! They have a type of fat called brown fat (which adults have far less of). Mitochondria in the fat process fuel in a way that makes extra heat and this helps to keep the baby warm.
2 b) If you go for a run your body gives off the heat of ten light bulbs. In seven minutes of playing squash you can make enough heat to boil one litre of water.

SQUASH?

NO, I'LL HAVE A CUP OF TEA, PLEASE!

3 a) Children's mitochondria are going at full blast making energy for an active lifestyle and a growing body. As a person gets older they slow down. And by the time they're as ancient as your more mature teachers, all their get up and go has got up and gone.
4 a) Overweight people often make *more* energy than thinner people (it takes a lot of energy to shift a big body). The idea that overweight people don't eat too much comes from surveys where overweight people have fibbed about their eating habits. Now you might think that fat people eat more because

they're greedy, but scientists have found that overweight people seem to take longer to feel full than thinner people.

5 b) Sorry, Harvey Tucker! Answer **a)** was suggested by US scientist Raymond Pearl (1879–1940) who wrote an article in 1927 entitled "Why lazy people live longest". But Pearl didn't take his own advice – he penned 700 articles and 17 books and he still lived to be 61.

6 b) If you fall asleep in your science test and start dreaming, your brain actually uses *more* energy than when you're awake! You may like to share this information with your teacher if she catches you sleeping during the test…

ZZZZ, HUH? OH ER, I'VE JUST BEEN POWERING UP MY BRAIN, MISS!

7 b) The brain needs glucose to make energy. Your blood contains just one hour's supply of glucose but your liver stores glucose in the form of a chemical called glycogen (gly-co-gen) to keep you going. But by morning your brain is hungry and it wants its glucose NOW! And that's why you feel tired and light-headed when you wake up. If you miss breakfast you might feel like a bike – two tyred to stand up – ha, ha.

TEACHER'S TEA-BREAK TEASER

At about 3 p.m. tap smartly on the staffroom door. When the door opens give your teacher a wide-awake smile and ask...

IS IT TRUE YOUR ENERGY LEVEL DROPS AT THIS TIME OF DAY?

MUMBLE, GROAN...

ANSWER

Yes it does. Scientist Robert Thayer of the University of California interviewed lots of people to check this.

Here's your teacher's day based on his findings…

7 am: Wake up feeling groggy…

11 am: Energy levels have increased…

3 pm: Energy levels low…

7 pm: Energy levels pick up.

11 pm: Energy levels dipping to bed-time

Tired people tend to be more bad-tempered and the best treatment is exercise. In fact, I should have warned you earlier…

HORRIBLE HEALTH WARNING!

Beware of KILLER TEACHERS! Yes, a tired teacher can be more dangerous than a tiger with toothache!

KILLER TEACHER GETTING MUCH NEEDED EXERCISE BY CHASING PUPIL.

Of course your teacher may try to revive themselves with a nice hot mug of tea. But inside that mug of tea something interesting is going on. The heat is spreading – it's heating up the cup, it's warming your teacher ... and eventually it'll warm up the rest of the universe.

What on Earth's going on...?

It's time to turn up the *heat*.

KILLER HEAT

Earlier we talked about cold (lack of heat energy) but now it's time for heat. Time for this book to warm up to its boiling, burning climax. Yes, it's time to get as hot as the hottest place in the universe! But first a question to fire your imagination...

HOW CAN HEAT SPREAD ACROSS THE COSMOS?

Whoops – that's a tricky one! We've asked Bernard Boyle back to answer your questions – let's hope he can keep his cool...

This makes the air or water lighter than the same amount of cold air or water. And so the hotter substance rises.

Shouldn't our teacher rise? He's full of hot air!

Finally, heat can spread through radiation.

RADIATION

Is that when people get zapped with high energy rays?

Well, yes but it's also a way that heat energy spreads in the form of a type of light that our eyes can't see. It's called infrared (in-fra-red) light.

INVISIBLE RAYS

It's what you're feeling when you feel hot in the sun. Now if you'll just turn to page 99 of my book...

That's right, INFRARED.

Did you say we're in for a read?

157

CONDUCTION IN ACTION

Conduction and insulation are so common I bet you come across them all the time. Yes, common as muck they are ... *and I can prove it!*

BET YOU NEVER KNEW!

Manure heaps steam in cold weather. The heat energy is actually made by billions of microbes cheerfully scoffing the delicious dung. But manure itself contains lots of air, water and bits of half-digested plants – all good insulators so that quite high temperatures can build up inside the heap until it's hot enough to steam. Fancy a steam in one?

BET YOU NEVER KNEW!

In the Second World War the Germans invaded Russia and in November 1941 they were poised to capture the Russian capital, Moscow. One night the temperature crashed. Thousands of soldiers were frost-bitten and their rotten feet had to be chopped off. The Germans wore boots shod with iron nails that conducted heat away from their feet. The Russians wore felt boots. Felt is a type of pressed wool. It's a good insulator and keeps the heat in. The Russians won and the Germans were left feeling sore about de-feet.

And talking about insulation...

DARE YOU DISCOVER ... WHAT A SOCK DOES TO ICE?

You will need:

A sunny windowsill or bright lamp • Sock (it doesn't have to be clean but you may feel cheesed off if it smells) • Two ice cubes • Two saucers • Gloves to protect fingers from ice

What you do:

1 Put on gloves. Place one ice cube on one saucer.

2 Put the other ice cube in the sock and wrap the sock around it tightly. Place the sock on the second saucer.

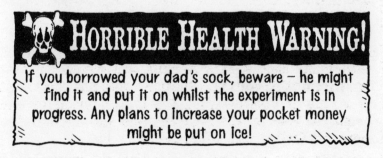

☠ HORRIBLE HEALTH WARNING!

If you borrowed your dad's sock, beware – he might find it and put it on whilst the experiment is in progress. Any plans to increase your pocket money might be put on ice!

3 Place the ice cube and the sock 15 cm from the light bulb.

YOU MAY NEED BOOKS TO RAISE THE ICE TO THE RIGHT HEIGHT.

HMMM! I SMELL CHEESE!

4 Leave the experiment for 45 minutes.

What do you notice?

a) Both ice cubes have melted.

b) The ice cube in the saucer has melted but the ice cube in the sock hasn't.

c) The ice cube in the sock has melted but not the ice cube in the saucer.

Result

b) The ice cube in the sock should be only half-melted. Like any material, the sock is a good insulator – but if an object is already cold the insulator can keep it cold too! Here's what happened:

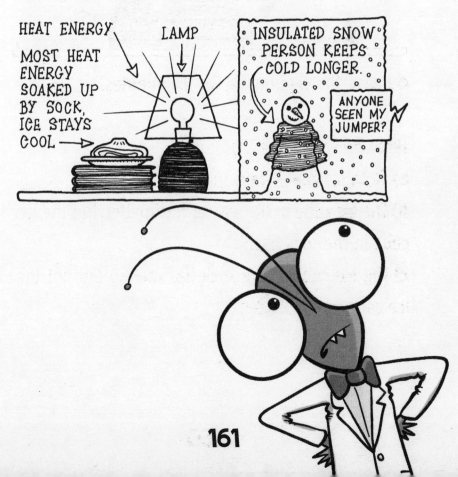

HEAT ENERGY

MOST HEAT ENERGY SOAKED UP BY SOCK, ICE STAYS COOL →

LAMP

INSULATED SNOW PERSON KEEPS COLD LONGER.

ANYONE SEEN MY JUMPER?

COULD YOU BE A SCIENTIST?

In 1960 the US Air Force carried out tests on volunteers to find out the greatest heat a human can survive. It turned out to be 260°C (500°F) — hotter than boiling water, hotter than a cooking steak. (I expect the volunteers were real hot-heads.) What were they wearing?

a) They were in the buff, raw, nip, nuddy or any other word that means that they wore no clothes.

b) A full set of clothing.

c) Flame proof underpants.

ANSWER

b) A person can stand 60°C (140°F) more heat when wearing clothes because the clothing insulates the skin from the heat.

Mind you, a heatwave can be as hot as a sauna. Killer heatwaves often strike the southern USA – in 1980, for example, thousands of people died as temperatures soared above 37.7°C (100°F). In Dallas, Texas the official in charge of stopping cruelty to children said:

IN THE PAST FEW WEEKS, MY CASELOAD HAS BEEN UP SUBSTANTIALLY... IF YOU'RE HOT YOU'RE GOING TO GET ANGRY FASTER.

Yes, I'm sorry to say that hot-tempered parents were taking it out on their children. So, BE WARNED. It's not a smart idea to ask for extra pocket money when your dad's sweltering.

But, talking about heatwaves, there's one place where the weather is *always* boiling. It's one of the hottest places on Earth – it's so hot that the heat kills people *all the time*. One early visitor called it:

THE NEAREST TO A LITTLE HELL ON EARTH THAT THE WHOLE WICKED WORLD CAN PRODUCE.

It's California's Death Valley and *Living on the Edge Magazine* was after a fearless, super-fit, ultra-brave reporter to write a feature on the region. They couldn't find one, and so...

HARVEY TUCKER'S BIG ADVENTURE

I was summoned to the editor's office but I had my excuses ready.

"I can't go!" I moaned. "Please don't send me back to the Arctic I'll get hypo-what's it and lose all my toes!"

The editor folded her arms and shook her head.

"Cut the cackle, greedy-guts. You're not going to the Arctic and you won't get hypothermia. Sunstroke, sunburn, fever maybe, but no hypothermia!"

And she gave me my next assignment - a feature on the effects of heat in Death Valley. "Death Valley" — it's the kind of name that gives me a cold shiver — or should I say a hot shudder?

But as my old dad used to say, we Tuckers are like a bad pork pie - you can't keep us down! So I thought, "No sweat — I'll just go and check out the scenery," and I threw myself into planning. (Well, for five minutes — then I watched the game on TV.) Then I packed my sunnies, 26 tubes of sunblock, 15 jars of suncream, my laptop, a crate of cold drinks and six family-sized boxes of ice-cream. That should keep me going! Then I dressed up in my home-made heat protection suit...

HERE'S ME IN MY HEAT CLOBBER!

SUNNIES

DRIP! DRIP!

STORMSTICK TO KEEP SUN OFF

WET SHEET TO KEEP MY BODY COOL - THAT GRIMGRAVE COBBER SAYS THAT AS THE WATER DRIES OFF IT TAKES HEAT ENERGY WITH IT - THAT'S WHY SWEATING COOLS YOU DOWN!

Day one: We Ozzies know about heat but this was something else! Phew! It was a stinker! Or 48.8° C (120° F) to be exact. I staggered to the salt lake — the hottest place in the valley. My sheet was bone dry in seconds. I was gagging for shade but there wasn't any, and what's more my ice-cream had melted!

I could feel my flesh sizzling like a burger on a barbie.

A quick squizz showed me the only life-forms were insects blown onto the lake — and me — and the insects didn't live long. I decided this place was real sticky — and so was I. So I huddled under my stormstick and had a go at some research. I downloaded some info from the Internet — but my laptop melted! So I took a gander at my book — maybe old Dr G has something more to say about heat...

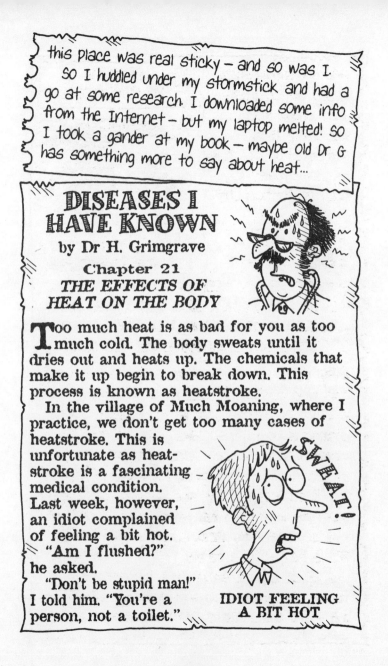

DISEASES I HAVE KNOWN

by Dr H. Grimgrave

Chapter 21
THE EFFECTS OF HEAT ON THE BODY

Too much heat is as bad for you as too much cold. The body sweats until it dries out and heats up. The chemicals that make it up begin to break down. This process is known as heatstroke.

In the village of Much Moaning, where I practice, we don't get too many cases of heatstroke. This is unfortunate as heatstroke is a fascinating medical condition. Last week, however, an idiot complained of feeling a bit hot.

"Am I flushed?" he asked.

"Don't be stupid man!" I told him. "You're a person, not a toilet."

SWEAT!

IDIOT FEELING A BIT HOT

The effects of heatstroke are easily summed up: fever, vomiting, headache, thirst, confusion, dry skin...

FEVER

HEADACHE

DRY SKIN

CONFUSION

THIRST

VOMITING

IDIOT WITH HEATSTROKE

...loss of consciousness and death.

So let that be a warming ... er ... *warning* to you. Sometimes the victim faints after feeling giddy.

In my days as an army doctor the soldiers would walk into lampposts during long, hot, marches. Their heart beat slowed and they couldn't pass water, or "urinate" as we doctors say.

The treatment is to rest in a cool place (I shut the soldiers in a cool food store) and drink lots of liquid. Water is the cheapest option, I find. Most doctors will tell you that victims of heatstroke should avoid hard work. Personally I take the view that hard work never killed anyone so I made them peel potatoes to make chips for my supper. It's a fried and tested remedy, ha ha.

"That's it" I thought "I'm crook, I've got heatstroke!" Just then I saw a sticky-beak scientist go swanning past — they study heat out here. She ordered me to drink 45 litres of water a day or my body would dry out! Too right — I was dripping with sweat. So I drank all my drinks — they were fizzy so I spent the next six hours burping.

At last I found a motel with air-conditioning. Heaven!

I jumped into my cozzie and dived into the pool and stayed there until sunset with just my nose sticking out of the water.

Days 2-10

Still recovering so I spent the next few days bludging by the pool — the motel had a nice line in ice-cold lager, cold slushy milkshakes and 64 flavours of ice-cream — ace tucker! (I felt I ought to sample them all to decide which I liked best.) I was sure the magazine wouldn't go to the knuckle about the bill!

SOME HOT NEWS JUST IN...

The Earth is heating up and causing killer climate chaos. There have been deadly droughts and fatal floods and the woeful warmth is melting ice from the land and raising sea levels and causing more floods. And here's why...

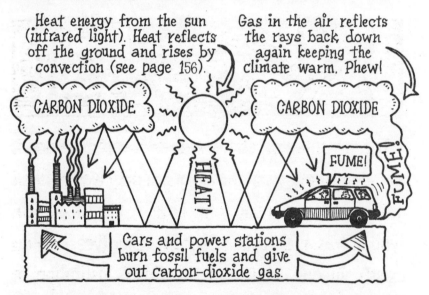

Heat energy from the sun (infrared light). Heat reflects off the ground and rises by convection (see page 156).

Gas in the air reflects the rays back down again keeping the climate warm. Phew!

CARBON DIOXIDE

CARBON DIOXIDE

HEAT!

FUME!

FUME!

Cars and power stations burn fossil fuels and give out carbon-dioxide gas.

This is sometimes known as the "greenhouse effect" because the gas traps heat like the glass of a greenhouse. OK – so any old science book will tell you this. But did you know that another gas causing global warming is methane? And a major cause of methane is farts – especially cows' farts (they blow-off more than humans) and also the farts of wood-eating insects called termites.

The greenhouse effect was discovered before it even became a problem. The possibility was pointed out by Irish scientist John Tyndall (1820–1893). Tyndall was a fantastic science teacher (yes, they do exist!). In one lecture at the Royal Institution in London he used the science of energy to play a cello … without touching it!

COULD YOU BE A SCIENTIST?

OK, so how did he manage that?
Was it...
a) Energy from
laser beams.
b) The
movement
energy of air
blasting from
an elephant's
trunk.

c) Sound energy travelling along a
pole from someone playing a piano in
the basement.

ANSWER
c) Sound energy passed along the
pole and moved the cello's strings.

Sadly, Tyndall was poisoned accidentally by his wife when she gave him too much of the medicine he was taking.

Mind you, in the next chapter you'll find killer temperatures that make global warming seem a bit chilly. Can't you just hear the crackling and roaring from the next few fiery pages…

It's gonna be HOT.

Is the fire brigade ready?

FEARSOME FIERY FURNACES

Put heat energy into something and three things can happen.

1 If it's solid it might melt into a liquid like Harvey's ice cream and his laptop a few pages ago.

2 If it's already a liquid it might turn into a gas — like water when it boils.

3 Or it might burst into flames

Scientists call the first two effects a "change in state". Basically what's going on is that heat energy is making the atoms wobble so fast they break free of neighbouring atoms. If they stick close to their neighbours the substance is a liquid – but if they go off in search of adventure they're a gas. YES!!! If you're an energetic, adventure-seeking atom life really is a gas!

Fire is different … actually the posh scientific word is combustion.

Killer energy fact file

Name: Combustion

Basic facts:

1 Take an object, throw in lots of oxygen very fast and mix them up with loads of heat energy and you get fire. (You can test your teacher by asking them how fires burned before oxygen was discovered, ha, ha.)

2 It's basically a chemical change and like any chemical change it can happen fast ... or slowly.

3 Fire takes stored chemical energy from the burning object and gives off heat energy and usually light energy too.

AN OBJECT   OXYGEN   HEAT   FLAMES & LIGHT

Killer details:

Humans like us weren't the first to use fire. A type of early human called *Homo erectus* used fire for cooking about 500,000 years ago. Scientists have found traces of their fires near Peking, China — so was this the first-ever Chinese takeaway?

And ever since we've been finding horrible uses for fire...

FIVE FATAL FIERY FACTS...

1 Burning alive was the punishment in many countries for opposing the Church or being a witch – Gerolamo Cardano nearly suffered this fate – remember? If the executioner felt kind they might smear the victim's body with a kind of fast-burning tar called pitch to finish them off faster.

2 In England women were burnt alive if they killed their husbands or clipped bits of silver off coins. The last woman to suffer this fate was Christian Murphy in 1789. A witness said:

She behaved with great decency, but was most shocked at the dreadful punishment she was about to undergo.

No wonder she was shocked – if she'd been a man she'd have got off with a nice quick hanging.

3 Burning wasn't the only method in which fire helped to get rid of people. In ancient China criminals were fried in oil. The English King Henry VIII (1491–1547) ordered that people found guilty of poisoning should be boiled alive.

4 Archaeologists have studied skeletons from Herculaneum, a Roman town destroyed by a volcano in AD 79. The people had been killed by superheated gases and the archaeologists found that their brains had boiled whilst they were *still alive*.

5 People who think that humans can burst into flames for unknown reasons (this is called spontaneous human combustion) have blamed the mystery fires on fart gases such as methane that burn easily. Scientists explain this burning question in terms of sparks from static electricity but either way it must be a nasty way to glow, er, go.

And now for more burning questions…

COULD YOU BE A SCIENTIST?

The human body burns at around 600–950°C (1,112–1,710°F) but some victims of spontaneous human combustion have been found burnt to ashes leaving their surroundings untouched.

How is this possible?

a) The fire was hot and quick-burning and burnt itself out.

b) The fire made the bodies explode from inside.

c) The fire burned like a candle, consuming the body's fat at high temperatures, but it didn't spread.

ANSWER

c) Non-fatty bits like the legs are often left amongst the ashes. In 1986 a scientist from Leeds University, England, set fire to a dead pig to produce similar results. Crispy bacon, anyone?

BET YOU NEVER KNEW!

It was once thought the victims were drunken people and the fires were made hot by alcohol burning inside them. So scientist Justus von Liebig (remember him from page 140?) tried soaking bits of dead body in alcohol and setting them on fire. They didn't burn. He then got rats drunk and set them on fire but they didn't burn either.

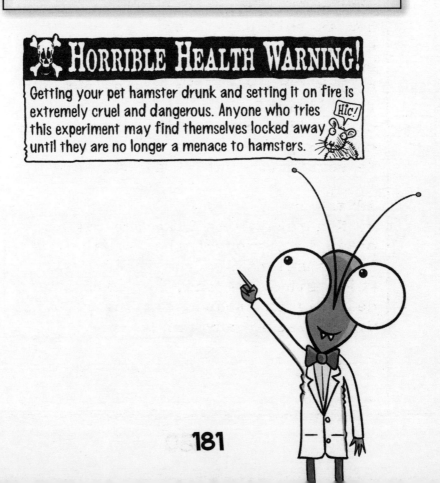

☠ HORRIBLE HEALTH WARNING!

Getting your pet hamster drunk and setting it on fire is extremely cruel and dangerous. Anyone who tries this experiment may find themselves locked away until they are no longer a menace to hamsters.

Hic!

COULD YOU BE A SCIENTIST?

In the Pacific Islands, India, Japan, Greece and many other parts of the world people do fire walking. They walk across glowing embers at 649°C (1200°F) in their bare feet without scorching their clothes or burning their feet.

How is this possible?

a) It's all to do with the conduction of heat.

b) They have flame-proof skin on their feet.

c) They're protected by magical charms.

182

a) The embers are carbon or stones which are poor conductors of heat. This slows the speed at which the heat gets to a walker's feet. The feet themselves are wet or sweaty and this also slows the heat. And the walkers usually move too quickly for their feet to burn. Mind you, it's still a brave feet ... er ... *feat.*

☠ HORRIBLE HEALTH WARNING!

Don't try anything like this – you might not be so lucky.

But talking about burning bodies – having recovered from his ordeal in Death Valley, Harvey Tucker is now facing his sternest challenge yet ... can he stand the *heat?*

HARVEY TUCKER'S BIG ADVENTURE

"I'm giving you one last chance, you wussy," snapped the editor. I guess she was feeling very hot under the collar about the huge bill that I had run up at the Cool 'n' Comfy Motel.

"You're going to report on the Fire Brigade training course or I'll clobber your lights! And this time there's going to be no telly, no Internet, no motels. Just you...."

"Just me?" I gulped.

"Yes – and I want your article about it on my desk next Tuesday or you won't be worth a burnt crumpet!"

"Where do I get a sick note?" I wondered.

Day one:

No sweat! All we did in the morning was sit on comfy chairs and listen to fire officers telling us about what to do in a fire. Nifty stuff like if your chip pan catches fire put a damp cloth over it and turn the power off. I could murder a plate of chips!

Lunch:

All this listening was hard work! I went to the canteen and ate six helpings of beans, sausages, eggs and, yes, chips. Fire-fighters are big eaters and even I was chockers!

184

Afternoon: Things got queasy in the arvo. The Fire Officer started blathering about burns and scalds. You've got to rinse them under cold running water and get medical advice if they're bad. Then he showed gross piccies of burn injuries. They're worse if the burn goes though the skin so there's no skin left. Also the heart and kidneys can shut down as blood moves towards the wound.

Then we looked at piccies of burned dead bods. Well, everyone else did — I covered my eyes. If you carry a burnt bod the guts can fall out and the arms and legs drop off.

I needed some air.

I took a dekko at the canteen to check out the tucker — sausages again. I left in a hurry clutching my mouth — I felt fit to chunder!

"Well, Harvey mate," I thought, "this is as bad as it gets."

I was wrong...

The Fire Officer announced that tomorrow we'd be tested on how to survive in a real burning building!!! What a choice — if I stuck the course I might catch fire — if I didn't I'd be fired anyway!

Day 2

The day started bad and that was the best bit...

"The main danger," said the Fire Officer, "is flashover or backdraft. Imagine an explosion of heat at $1000°$ C ($1832°$ F). It's hot enough to burn the clothes off your back and split your bones open. It's so hot that even a jet of water from a hose turns to steam."

I imagined it – and closed my eyes and tried to think of food. This usually calms me down but for some reason I started thinking about flaming Xmas puds!

After a real 'mis' hour of waiting and ten visits to the dunny it was my turn. At the training school they have a real-sized building that they stage training fires in. I found myself in the bedroom...

"Close the door!" yelled the Fire Officer through his megaphone.

I did as I was told but smoke began to ooze under the door.

"Block the gap with a wet towel!" he instructed.

I found a towel – it was dry so I called for help.

"There's a tap in the basin!"

"I can't see it – there's too much smoke!" I yelled.

It's true I couldn't even see my fingers. But then I found the tap – I wet the towel and stuffed it under the door. Then I wet myself – with water from the tap, you'll understand. I thought it might stop me bursting into flames.

SPLASH! "Get out of the building, Tucker!" barked the Fire Officer.

I crawled to the window and looked down. The ground seemed a long way off.

"Now what?" I called anxiously.

"Throw some bedding out the window and jump!"

I did as I was told — well, all except the last bit.

"What are you waiting for, you lily-livered drongo?!" yelled the Fire Officer, coming close in order to see through the smoke that was (despite my efforts) gushing out the window.

I couldn't answer because I was spluttering.

So I jumped. It was easy and it helped that the Fire Officer was there to catch me. Well, I'm not sure he meant to catch me but he should be out of hospital in the next few weeks...

GETTING HOTTER...

If there's one thing worse than a flashover, it's a firestorm. A huge killer fire that sucks air from its surroundings in hurricane-force gusts and sucks in humans too. Temperatures can reach 800°C (1472°F) – hot enough to melt glass and lead. And the heat is enough to spread the fire as houses nearby get so hot they burst into flames. And the fire consumes all the air in the area and kills anyone who isn't burnt to death.

But a firestorm is not the hottest temperature you can get by any stretch. It's *nothing* compared to the heat belted out every day by our friendly neighbourhood star...

Killer energy fact file

Name: The sun's energy

Basic facts:

1 The sun's super-hot core is about 15 MILLION°C and even its surface is a rather sweaty 5,500°C.

2 Inside the core the sun's gigantic gravity squishes hydrogen protons (protons = specks of matter that make up atoms) together to form helium. Some matter is turned into energy and escapes as heat and light.

3 In 1994 US scientists used the same process to heat atoms to 510 MILLION°C. But that's nothing. In 2006 US scientists used an X-ray blasting machine to cook tungsten atoms to 2 BILLION°C. Those scientists were hot stuff!

Killer details:

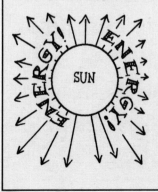

1 The sun makes thousands of times more energy than we need. There's *twice* as much energy in the sunshine that falls on the roads of the USA in a year than all the gas and oil and coal burnt in the world in that time.

2 We only get 0.00000005% or five parts in every hundred million of the sun's energy. The rest of this killer energy blasts away into space.

THE SUN SOUNDS PRETTY AWESOME – DOESN'T IT?

Well, it's nothing special. Just an average star amongst at least 170 billion stars in an average galaxy amongst at least 170 billion galaxies in the known universe. For REAL energy you need to go back to the Big Bang. That's when the universe started about 13.8 billion years ago.

All the energy in the universe was stuffed into a tiny dot smaller than an atom. And it was so hot no one can possibly say how hot it was. Even after it had cooled a bit it was still 10,000 million million million million degrees. Lucky humans weren't around then or we'd have stood less chance than a baby budgie on a cat's cookery course. Meanwhile this dot started to get bigger and bigger and BIGGER and it still hasn't stopped ... and now it's the universe!

LIFE-SIZE SKETCH OF UNIVERSE DURING THE BIG BANG

Remember the First Law of Thermodynamics? It says that energy can't be lost but that heat can turn into movement energy. Well, all the energy you can think of, all the energy of animals and electricity, the energy in your muscles and your beating heart, first came into being with the Big Bang. And you can listen to the Big Bang on your radio any time you want. No really, you can!

DARE YOU DISCOVER ... HOW TO LISTEN TO THE BIG BANG ON RADIO?

You will need:

• An old radio that you have to tune (not a digital radio)

What you do:

1 Switch on the radio.

2 Make sure it's not tuned to any radio station.

What do you hear?

a) Strange alien voices – YIKES! They're planning to invade Earth!

b) A steady roar like a distant explosion.

c) Crackling, popping and hissing sounds.

c) Nearly all these sounds are made on Earth. Lightning strikes or electrical equipment make most sounds, but a few could be made by microwaves. (This is the energy that zaps a milky bar in a microwave oven.) Some of these microwaves are the remains of energy from the Big Bang.

Just imagine – the microwaves drifted forever through the cold darkness of space and they ended up in your radio! Who says radio is boring? And so we end this chapter with…

Didn't you say on page 8 that you were going to tell us the fate of the universe?

THAT VERY ALERT READER FROM PAGE 125

Oh, I'm sorry it must have slipped my mind! Well, it's just a small detail but the ultimate fate of the universe is…

OOPS – sorry readers we seem to have run out of space for this chapter – you'll have to read on to find out…

A POWER FOR GOOD?

The Energy Monster is everywhere. It's in the singing of birds and the swaying of grass. It makes you warm and comfortable but it shows its killer powers in a raging fire. It's in the turning of the pages of this book and every wisp of steam from a kettle. Energy is the pulse of the universe and without it the universe would die.

The Big Bang and the Laws of Thermodynamics supply clues about the future. In particular there's a miserable message in the Second Law – yes, the one about heat energy always being lost. Here's how Scottish scientist James Clerk Maxwell (1831–1879) summed it up:

If you throw a tumblerful of water into the sea you cannot get the same tumbler of water back again.

Sounds reasonable – and if you don't believe me you can always try it next time you're at the seaside...

WHERE'S MY DRINK?

What Maxwell was saying was that the amount of confusion and muddle in the universe is always growing. It's like drops of water mixing in the sea and it'll *never* sort itself out on its own. It makes sense. Think of your bedroom – I bet you it *never* tidies itself on its own!

Now look at energy. The universe started off as a tidy little dot of energy all squashed neatly in one place. But now it's an untidy hotch-potch of hot stars and cold space and it's getting worse. The Second Law says that energy is always getting lost in the form of heat energy. So where does all this heat energy go? Well, the Second Law has the answer: heat always heads for the coldest place it can find – and that, ultimately, is outer space.

And once heat energy drifts off into space no one can ever get it back – never, ever, ever. And that means one day all the energy in the universe will have turned to heat and floated off into space. The stars will sputter out like candle flames and the planets will die of cold. Eventually even the dusty remains of the stars and planets will turn to heat energy and drift away.

The universe will be a thin cold soup of tiny bits of atoms floating about in the dark emptiness. Time will go on but nothing will ever change, and nothing will ever happen again. It'll be worse than a wet winter weekend when the telly's broken down.

SPOT THE DIFFERENCE COMPETITION

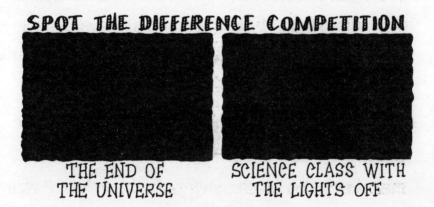

THE END OF
THE UNIVERSE

SCIENCE CLASS WITH
THE LIGHTS OFF

And in the end the loss of its energy will kill the universe – if it doesn't die of boredom first!

But let's look on the bright side. For one thing, it's not going to happen before the weekend. Scientists think it will take about 1,000,000,000,000,000, 000,000,000,000,000 (one thousand billion billion billion) years so they've got plenty of time to find a way to get the heat energy back or perhaps find a nice new universe for us to live in.

Or we might discover a new kind of power. People who believe that UFOs are alien spacecraft claim that they might work through some kind of anti-gravity force. This would have to get its energy from somewhere, and perhaps one day we'll find out…

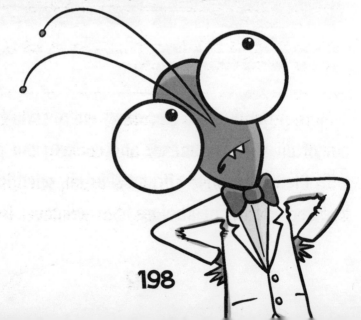

BET YOU NEVER KNEW!

In 1878 inventor Thomas Edison (1847–1931) wanted to invent anti-gravity underwear that floated around in mid-air! A drawing of the time shows a dad towing his floating children.

But wait, would YOU fancy turning up at school in a pair of ground-defying knickers?

More urgently (and seriously) we're still running out of oil and gas energy and cooking our planet with the greenhouse effect. As usual, scientists are thinking up lots of answers, but whatever is done it's bound to involve developing renewable forms of energy like the sun's power and geothermal, wind and wave energy. These aren't going to run out like fossil fuels and don't give off gases that cause global warming.

But as the world fills up with people and more people travel in space we're going to need lots more energy. So here are some possibilities for the future...

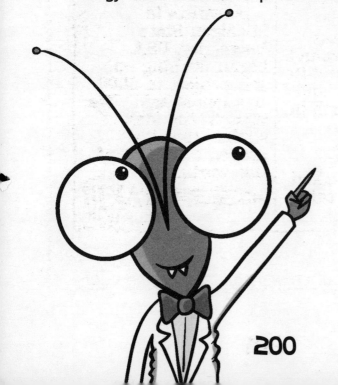

SUPER-SUN SATELLITE SOARS!

Scientists are thrilled at the success of a giant satellite going round the sun. The satellite picks up power and beams it to Earth in the form of microwave rays. Said one beaming boffin, "We've taken a real shine to this project!"

POO POWERS PLANET PROBE!

It was revealed today that the interplanetary spacecraft is powered by fuel cells fuelled by germs eating rotting astronauts' poo.

Scientists in Michigan State University, USA began working on this project in 2000. A scientist said, "We thought the idea stinks – but it's proved to be out of this world."

FART!

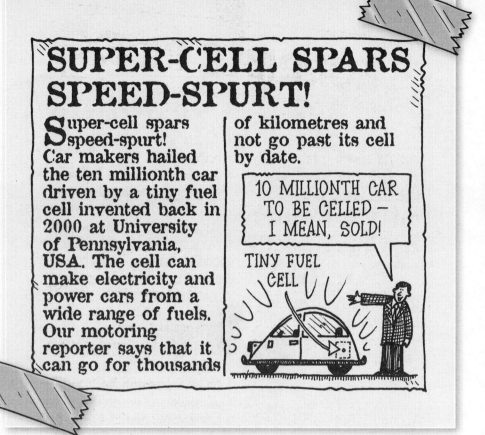

SUPER-CELL SPARS SPEED-SPURT!

Super-cell spars speed-spurt! Car makers hailed the ten millionth car driven by a tiny fuel cell invented back in 2000 at University of Pennsylvania, USA. The cell can make electricity and power cars from a wide range of fuels. Our motoring reporter says that it can go for thousands of kilometres and not go past its cell by date.

10 MILLIONTH CAR TO BE CELLED — I MEAN, SOLD!

TINY FUEL CELL

One thing's for sure: science has come a long way in understanding energy. And perhaps one day human cleverness will find a way of turning killer energy into a power for good.

HORRIBLE INDEX

absolute zero (absolutely freezing) 21, 39, 54–6
alchemists, alarming 87–9
Amundsen, Roald (Norwegian explorer) 80
Anaxagoras (Greek philosopher) 14
archaeologists, archaic 178
Aristotle (Greek philoopher) 14
atoms, tiny 39, 46–7, 55–6, 67, 91, 101, 156, 175, 189–90
ATP (chemical energy store) 143–4, 146

backdraft (heat explosions) 185–8
bananas 9–10, 104
bellies, bulging 9–10, 89
Bessler, Johann (German scientist) 130–2
Big Bang 190–4
blisters 73, 101
blood, draining 22–7, 64–5

body bits 133–54
Boulton, Matthew (British factory owner) 98–100

candles, creepy 84–5, 91, 180
Cardano, Gerolamo (Italian scientist) 128–9, 177
Carnot, Nicolas (French scientist) 125
cells, secret 140–5
Celsius, Anders (Swiss scientist) 50–1, 55
coal 55, 81, 92–3, 96, 99–100, 117, 189
combustion (fire) 175–6, 179–80
conduction (heat moving) 156, 158–61, 182–3
convection (heat rising) 156, 170
cramp, excruciating 144
cryogenics (deep-freezing) 59, 61, 71

Da Vinci, Leonardo (Italian scientist) 128
dance, dying to 136–8
dandruff 39
dead bodies, preserving 39, 58–62
Death Valley 164–7, 183

Edison, Thomas (American inventor) 199
electricity 13, 54, 56, 85, 92, 94, 101–2, 106, 119, 179, 191, 193, 202
experiments, endless 28, 30–5, 44–7, 56, 87, 96, 159–61, 192–3
explorers, intrepid 70, 76, 78–80

fact files, fascinating 11–13, 18, 39, 67, 101, 134, 146–7, 176, 189
Fahrenheit, Daniel (German scientist) 43, 49–50
farts, flaming 7, 171, 179
fat 7, 78–9, 85, 87, 89, 151, 180
firestorms 188
firewalking 182–3
First Law of Thermodynamics 20, 22, 27–8, 30–1, 34, 116, 191
flashovers (heat explosions) 185–8
food energy 139–40
fossil fuels, filthy 92–4, 100, 200
friction (rubbing force) 56, 106, 127
fridges, frosty 69–70
frostbite, freezing 73–7, 158
fuel, foul 84–6

galaxies, far, far away 37, 190
Galilei, Galileo (Italian scientist) 42, 48
gas 81, 92–3, 95–7, 99–100, 170, 174–5, 178–9, 189, 199–200
geothermal power (Earth energy) 104–6, 200
germs, grisly 60, 72, 134, 201
global warming 171, 173, 200
glucose (sugar) 142–3, 151–2
gold, greed for 87–8
greenhouse effect, ghastly 170–1, 199
Guericke, Otto von (German scientist) 43

heat energy, heaps of 12, 18–21, 26–7, 29, 34–51, 60–3, 67–8, 70, 77, 80, 85, 94, 97, 101, 103, 106, 109, 115–16, 126, 155–76, 189, 191, 196, 198
heatstroke, horrific 167–9
heatwaves, hateful 163–4
helium (gas) 57, 189
Hero of Alexandria (Greek engineer) 113
hypothermia (chronic chilling) 74–5, 165

ice hotels 65–6
infrared (invisible light) 157
insulation (heat stopping) 156, 158–62

Joule, James (British scientist) 28–9, 120
joules (energy measure) 29

Kelvin, Lord (British scientist) 53–5
kinetic energy, killer 108–9

Lagrange, Joseph-Louis (French scientist) 140
Lavoisier, Antoine (French chemist) 139–40

Laws of Thermodynamics, lousy 16–38, 52, 54, 68, 116, 130, 191, 194, 196
Leibniz, Gottfried (German philosopher) 14
Liebig, Justus von (German scientist) 140, 181
light 13, 85, 91, 97, 103, 176, 189

machines, magic 109, 112–17
magnetism 13, 56, 94
matches 85–6
Maxim, Hiram (American inventor) 119
Maxwell, James Clerk (Scottish scientist) 194–5
Mayer, Julius von (German doctor) 22–30
mega-tsunamis 109–11
mercury (moving metal) 43
methane (farting gas) 171, 179
microwave ovens 193
mines, miserable 116
mitochondria, making energy 142–5, 147, 150
mountaineers, madcap 77
movement energy, mighty 12, 20, 26–7, 29, 34, 106–32, 134, 139, 146, 191

Murdock, William (Scottish inventor) 96–100, 118
muscles, amazing 139–40, 143–4, 146–54, 191

Newcomen, Thomas (English inventor) 116, 118
nitrogen 57–8, 60, 62
North Pole 50, 76–7, 79
northern lights (natural light show) 50
nuclear power, no thanks 101

oil, oozing 81, 92–4, 96, 100, 102–3, 178, 189, 199
oxygen (breathing gas) 25–6, 73, 91, 143–4, 176

Parsons, Charles (Irish inventor) 120–4
pee 56, 144
perpetual motion, impossible 124–31
petrol, putrid 9–10, 81, 94
phosphorus (glowing chemical) 86–91, 144
pistons, impressive 117
poo 201
potential energy, powerful 12–13, 83

Prévost, Pierre (Swiss scientist) 40

quizzes, quick 102–3, 148–52

radiation (killer rays) 101, 157
rats, drunken 7, 181
renewable energy 103, 200
rocks, hot 96, 104–5
Royal Society (British science club) 30, 41

sausages 35, 48, 184–5
Savery, Thomas (English engineer) 114, 116
scales, serious 48–51, 55
scientists, several 7, 13–16, 18, 21–30, 40–3, 48, 50–6, 67, 80, 95, 100, 115–16, 124–6, 129–31, 139–40, 142–4, 151, 156, 162, 169, 172, 175–6, 179–82, 189, 194, 199, 201
Scott, Robert Falcon (British explorer) 80
seances (ghostly gatherings) 91
Second Law of Thermodynamics 20, 22, 35–8, 54, 68, 194, 196
snot 72
snowballs 67
solar power 103, 200

sound 13, 70, 112, 172, 192–3
South Pole 76–8, 80
Stahl, Georg Ernst (German scientist) 14
steam 9, 94, 98–9, 101, 113–14, 117–21, 158, 186, 194
steam engines, improved 116–18, 121–2, 125
stenching, smelly 95
stored energy 11, 81–4, 134, 139, 146, 176
sun 20, 55–6, 103, 157, 165, 169–70, 189–91, 200–1
surgeons, stitching 64–5

teachers, teasing 28–9, 68, 82, 91, 93, 152–4, 176
thermometers, tacky 41–3
thermoscopes (old thermometers) 42–6, 48
Third Law of Thermodynamics 21–2, 52, 54
Thompson, Benjamin (American scientist) 40–1
tidal power 103
toes, falling off 73–7, 165
Trevithick, Richard (English inventor) 118–19
turbines, terrific 94, 101, 119, 121, 123

Tyndall, Johm (Irish scientist) 171, 173

universe, fate of 8, 35–7, 154–5, 190, 193–8
uranium (radiactive metal) 101

volcanoes, vile 9–10, 105, 178

Watt, James (Scottish engineer) 99, 116–17
wave power, wonderful 103, 200
wee, rotting 87–90, 144
wind power 103, 127, 200
wood 84, 98